Praise for *Playfu*

"*Playful Intelligence* is one of the most important and influential books you will ever read. It struck me on a deeply personal and emotional level. Anthony DeBenedet has written a wonderful and practical guide to being a more effective parent, spouse, friend, and colleague; it's a new way to think about what matters most in work and life. Simply put, this book will make you a better human being. Prepare to be inspired!"

—Tom Rath, best-selling author of *StrengthsFinder 2.0*,
How Full is Your Bucket?, and *Wellbeing*

"Anthony DeBenedet's timely work shows us how playfulness makes us better and offers a simple framework for integrating playfulness into our day-to-day lives. An antidote to the pressure, seriousness, and responsibility overload that defines much of adulthood, *Playful Intelligence* is the perfect prescription for our high-stress lives."

—Jonah Berger, best-selling author of *Contagious*
and *Invisible Influence*

"By breaking playfulness down into its component parts, DeBenedet invites us on a delightful adventure filled with compelling research, inspiring stories, and practical steps that makes it possible for us to cultivate this elusive quality and unleash it into our daily lives. In other words, he provides our magical inner child with an escape route through the thicket of our adult conditioning. The world just became a more humane and playful place!"

—Gwen Gordon, Emmy award-winning creative director
and author of *The Wonderful W*

"Anthony's own playful intelligence shines through every page of this delightful and thought-provoking book. His real gift, however, is showing the rest of us how to be more playful in our adult lives. If everyone took the guidance in this book to heart, the world would be a much better place!"

—Lawrence J. Cohen, Ph.D., author of *Playful Parenting*

"*Playful Intelligence* is exactly what the doctor ordered! In his new book, DeBenedet beautifully combines his expertise as a physician, behavioral-science aficionado, and fun-loving human being, and writes us the perfect prescription for a happier, healthier, and more playfully engaged life. By breaking down playfulness into its five key components, and sharing ways to incorporate the power of play into our everyday lives, this book gives adults the permission they need to work hard, and play harder."

—Meredith Sinclair, M. Ed., lifestyle expert and author of
*Well Played: The Ultimate Guide to Awakening
Your Family's Playful Spirit*

"It happens only rarely that I come across a book which inspires, gives me goosebumps, and makes me cry. Dr. Anthony DeBenedet has done it with *Playful Intelligence*. DeBenedet shows us why playfulness should live at the core of our adult lives to balance out the more serious parts. One of the most precious points that DeBenedet puts forward is that playfulness is at the heart of resiliency and our ability to bounce back from challenging and stressful experiences. Insight like this, and so much more, is what makes this book a powerful invitation and permission slip to see life through the eyes of a child, while constantly connecting to the wisdom harvested in our own experiences and throughout generations. Highly recommended and inspiring for all areas of life!"

—Anette Prehn, social scientist (MA),
pioneer in applied neuroscience,
and author of *Play Your Brain* and the *Brain Friends* series

"*Playful Intelligence* is just what the doctor ordered for so many of us who are living stressful lives. Dr. DeBenedet mixes humor, science, and poignant real-life stories to create a book that reminds us to laugh, to daydream, to live in the moment, and, ultimately, to love."

—Sanjay Saint, M.D., M.P.H., Chief of Medicine,
VA Ann Arbor Healthcare System; George Dock Professor of
Internal Medicine at the University of Michigan

Playful Intelligence

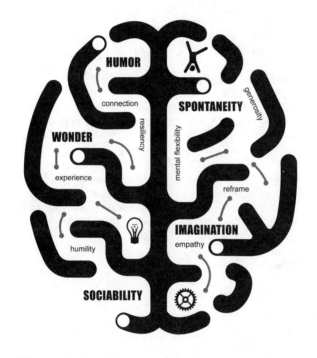

The Power of *Living Lightly* in a Serious World

Anthony T. DeBenedet, M.D.

SANTA
MONICA
PRESS

Published by:

Santa Monica Press LLC
P.O. Box 850
Solana Beach, CA 92075
1-800-784-9553
www.santamonicapress.com
books@santamonicapress.com

S A N T A
M O N I C A
P R E S S

Printed in the United States

Santa Monica Press books are available at special quantity discounts when purchased in bulk by corporations, organizations, or groups. Please call our Special Sales department at 1-800-784-9553.

This book is intended to provide general information. The publisher, author, distributor, and copyright owner are not engaged in rendering professional advice or services. The publisher, author, distributor, and copyright owner are not liable or responsible to any person or group with respect to any loss, illness, or injury caused or alleged to be caused by the information found in this book.

ISBN-13 978-1-59580-085-5

Library of Congress Cataloging-in-Publication Data

Names: DeBenedet, Anthony T., author.
Title: Playful intelligence : the power of living lightly in a serious world
  / Anthony T. DeBenedet, M.D.
Description: Solana Beach, CA : Santa Monica Press, [2018] | Includes
  bibliographical references. |
Identifiers: LCCN 2017055034 (print) | LCCN 2017058755 (ebook) |
ISBN
  9781595807939 () | ISBN 9781595800855
Subjects: LCSH: Play. | Imagination. | Stress (Psychology)
Classification: LCC BF717 (ebook) | LCC BF717 .D394 2018 (print) |
DDC
  153.3--dc23
LC record available at https://lccn.loc.gov/2017055034

Cover and interior design and production by Future Studio
Front cover image courtesy of Pongsuwan/Creative Market

For Anna . . .

and Ava, Mia, and Lola—down the road

Contents

INTRODUCTION: *Restore Joyland* 9

CHAPTER ONE: *Imagination* 17

    Imagination Well Played

        Reframe Readiness 50

        Empathize with Your Enemy 51

        What a Day for a Daydream 53

CHAPTER TWO: *Sociability* 55

    Sociability Well Played

        Anchors Aweigh 94

        Powerless Communication 95

CHAPTER THREE: *Humor* 99

    Humor Well Played

        Connection 143

        Resiliency 145

CHAPTER FOUR: *Spontaneity* 147

    Spontaneity Well Played

        Finding Flexibility 194

        The Generosity Hurdle 196

CHAPTER FIVE: *Wonder* 199

    Wonder Well Played
      Wonder Rehab 229

CONCLUSION: *The Rainbow Hallway* 233

Acknowledgments 243
Notes 247
About the Author 263

INTRODUCTION

Restore Joyland

A s a child growing up in the 1960s, Marlene Irvin took many trips to Joyland, an amusement park in her hometown of Wichita, Kansas. Goose bumps would sprout on her arms the moment her family drove into Joyland's parking lot. "The carousel circling at the entrance to the park was always the highlight for me," Marlene said. "I could watch the horses for hours."

Joyland certainly made a lasting impression on Marlene, as she got her "first real job" at Wichita's Chance Manufacturing, the largest manufacturer of amusement park rides in the world at the time. Marlene started in the fiberglass shop, where the carousel horses' frames, along with parts for Ferris wheels, roller coasters, and other rides, were pieced together. She eventually found her way to Chance's art and decoration department, becoming one of the lead horse artists. Then, in 1992, after working at Chance for nearly fifteen years, Marlene decided to start her own business, focusing exclusively on carousel restoration.

Coincidentally, around this time, Joyland started experiencing a decline in attendance. In 2006, to the heartbreak of Wichitans young and old, Joyland shut down after more than fifty years of operation. Local preservation organizations purchased some of the park's artifacts, and Joyland's thirty-six carousel horses were donated to Botanica, a Wichita-owned botanical gardens. Botanica asked Marlene to restore the deteriorated horses, and she accepted the challenge.

As Marlene finished each horse, Botanica displayed them for the public to see. Although they looked different compared to their glory days at Joyland, thanks to Marlene's artistic efforts, the horses impressed observers even more than they had before. When native Wichitans saw them, their most common question was: "Will we be able to ride them?" Even as adults, they remembered riding the horses at Joyland when they were kids.

Marlene always smiled and answered: "They've been waiting for you to come back."

●━━●

If you've picked up this book, you're probably someone who senses that adulthood—at least the way most of us are experiencing it—is missing something. Put another way, you detect how the good of your middle years sometimes feels eclipsed by the stress of them.

The good unfolds in various ways. Loving someone deeper than you ever thought was possible. Witnessing a child's joy. Feeling a friend's unconditional support. Discovering your purpose.

But so does the stress. Learning the work of marriage. Crossing the bumpy terrain of parenting. Determining which social relationships click. Facing grave hardship. Finding contentment in your career. When the stress overshadows the good, adulthood starts to feel overwhelming. And pretty soon you find yourself doing everything you can to endure your middle years, while wondering whether you're actually enjoying them.

This is exactly where I was five years ago. In the wake of accelerating responsibilities, my life was becoming more intense and stressful. My relationships, clinical work as a physician, and basic interactions with the world were blurring into a frazzled mosaic. Going through the motions became my norm, and every day brought busyness and exhaustion.

I thought about whether I was depressed. I didn't think I was. Anxious? Sure, but aren't we all anxious on some level? I also thought about the lifestyle factors that I would discuss with my patients. Was I getting enough sleep? Was I exercising regularly? Was I eating healthy? Was I making time for fun?

On average, I was doing okay in these areas, but the last one about fun caught my attention. I didn't feel short on fun, yet questioning myself made me think about the differences between childhood and adulthood when it comes to fun and play. I thought about how children live in a constant state of play, whereas adults live in a constant state of trying to keep up. The endless pressure to stay on top of our responsibilities seems to stack our decks toward serious and stressful living. I fully realized that adulthood, in general, was more stressful than childhood. I also knew that it sometimes demanded seriousness of the highest order. But stress and seriousness seemed to have a monopoly on adult life, especially mine.

Was the intensity of adulthood causing me to make less time for fun? It didn't feel this way to me, nor did it seem to be true in the lives of the adults I knew. Then came a realization: maybe it wasn't play or fun that stress cut into, but rather the playful part of our personalities. As the intensity of adulthood grows, perhaps the playfulness that's inside of us erodes. In other words, the playful part of our personalities—our internal Joylands, if you will—begins to wither away, and we start to abandon the part of ourselves that sees the world as an amusement park.

My life was barreling toward burnout, numbness was setting in, and the net effect seemed to be a decay of the playful aspect of my personality. To use a cartoon metaphor, I needed Jiminy Cricket—a wise and comical partner—to come alive inside my mind and help me live out an important truth: it's not about taking life less seriously, but rather taking *ourselves* less seriously, in a smart way.

Which brought me to this book, and perhaps brought you as well. We can reclaim our middle years by learning how to live lightly, as we navigate the seriousness of adulthood. That said, you won't find a bunch of games and activities within these pages. I assume you are already having as much fun as you can in the limited leisure time we are given. What I hope to convey is that at this point in your life, it's just as important to think about playfulness as it is to play.

Let's look at the difference between the two for a moment.

Play is an action. Playfulness is a behavior (or a set of behaviors). Play is the act of throwing horseshoes in your backyard. Playfulness is an inclination to smile or laugh while you're doing it (unlike your Uncle Myron, who takes it way too seriously). One playful family I know often tells the story of their first trip to the circus—an act of play. Excited to capture the memory of their family outing, the parents ushered their children to a stage where families could have their picture taken with clowns. As the family stepped onto the stage, the youngest son burst into tears. Everyone—the parents and siblings, as well as the clowns and photographer—tried to calm him, but to no avail. Then the mother shouted, "Quick, let's do grumpy faces!" Everyone frowned happily as the photographer snapped the photo—an act of playfulness.

Acts of play come easy, and most adult lives aren't missing them. Jump-starting the playful part of our personalities is harder. This requires intentional thought about playfulness, as well as knowledge of how it makes our lives better. That's why the title of this book is *Playful Intelligence.*

From an intelligence theory perspective, playful intelligence is not a radical new form of intelligence. Rather, it's an extension of both intrapersonal and interpersonal intelligence, which have been described by Howard Gardner, an American developmental psychologist best known for his theory of multiple intelligences. Intrapersonal intelligence is knowledge of the internal aspects, the feelings, emotions, and behaviors of oneself; interpersonal intelligence is knowledge of others' moods, temperaments, motivations, and intentions. Bringing these concepts together, playful intelligence is the notion of knowing how playfulness can influence one's inner and outer adult life.

When I first started thinking about adult playfulness, I scoured the scientific literature to learn how others have studied it. Unlike research on playfulness in children, research on playfulness in adults is limited. The studies that do exist, however, have appropriately examined behavioral qualities that are commonly associated with playfulness: being adventurous, creative, energetic, humorous, imaginative, outgoing, sociable, spontaneous, and many more. Nearly forty qualities have been linked to adult playfulness.

As I thought about each quality, my first conclusion was that for someone to revive the playful part of his or her personality, he or she needed to think about these qualities individually; for it must be true that playfulness, like anything else, is best understood as a function of its parts. For example, say that you are on your lunch break. While you are walking down the street, heading to your staple sandwich shop, you suddenly decide that today you're going to seek a culinary adventure. You see a quaint Korean café and step in. You try some pork bulgogi and kimchi stew, and they are delicious. You'll be back! To best understand how playfulness worked here, it's important to recognize the input from both the playful quality of being adventurous (in this scenario, a cuisine adventure) and the playful quality of spontaneity—as, on a whim, you veered from your sandwich routine.

My second conclusion was that if I was going to explore these qualities one by one, and investigate how each one influenced my life as well as the lives of others, forty was too many for me to wrap my head around. I needed to whittle the list down to five—the five that carried the most influence.

So I began a quest to determine which five playful qualities, in the right doses and contexts, can help us rediscover our playgrounds, and, in turn, live our best lives. Along my journey, I've observed, studied, and interviewed hundreds of people—many of whom are my patients. I've also conducted a broad search across a range of disciplines—notably psychology, sociology, history, neuroscience, and economics—to untangle the profound and unexpected ways that playfulness impacts adult life.

Fortunately, the five qualities of high value emerged quickly: *imagination, sociability, humor, spontaneity,* and *wonder.* We all have the capacity to use these playful qualities in our daily lives, but we usually don't do so consciously. We also rarely think about the influence they can have on our overall happiness and well-being.

The core chapters of this book are built on these five qualities, along with case studies to illustrate each one. At the end of each chapter is a short section called "Well Played." Here you will find practical tips for using the main points of the chapter in everyday life. The result, I hope, is a representation of how adulthood—from health and relationships to difficult situations and professional success—benefits from engaging with the five playful qualities studied here. And the bigger result—my wish, you could say—is that your story will be bettered after reading this book.

As Jiminy Cricket once said, "The most fantastic, magical things can happen, and it all starts with a wish."

CHAPTER ONE

Imagination

Salvatore Maddi first learned about stress theory while he was earning his doctorate in psychology at Harvard in the 1950s. Henry Murray, one of Sal's professors, studied personalities. Murray believed that our personalities determined how we respond to stress. Sal, like many of Murray's other students, was inspired by the intersection of personality and stress that Murray was investigating—so much so that he chose to continue exploring the connection after graduate school.

Sal joined the faculty of the psychology department at the University of Chicago. Besides his research and teaching roles, he worked as a consultant for the Illinois Bell Telephone Company, advising the company on how personality qualities influenced aspects of the work experience, from collegiality to solving problems and being productive.

At the time, Illinois Bell was one of multiple "Baby Bells" in the United States that was controlled by the American Telephone and Telegraph Company (AT&T),

which had been the only provider of telephone services in the United States since 1877. The federal government had been working hard to break up AT&T for many years. By the 1970s, an AT&T divestiture seemed inevitable. Naturally, this caused a great deal of stress for Baby Bell employees, including those at Illinois Bell. From the top of the ladder down, every Illinois Bell employee knew that AT&T's impending divestiture would bring sweeping organizational changes, layoffs, and corporate uncertainty. Sal knew it, too. But he also saw the corporate upheaval as an opportunity to learn how differences in personality affected how people managed stress.

In 1975, with the cooperation of Illinois Bell's workforce, Sal and his research team began a twelve-year longitudinal study on personality and stress funded by Illinois Bell and the National Institutes of Health. The project involved nearly 260 Illinois Bell employees. The participants went through numerous medical examinations, psychological interviews, and performance reviews over the course of the study. Every aspect of their health was carefully monitored and scrutinized. Their approaches to stress were meticulously documented and analyzed.

The first five years of the study, the period when stress was moderate but not overwhelming, provided baseline data on all the participants. This proved critical to the research, as the stress level rose considerably in year six (1981) when the United States Justice Department ordered AT&T to undergo divestiture. Teams that had been together for years changed overnight, only to change again a week later, and then again the following week.

Every month, there were new bosses in the office, and for many months, layoffs occurred daily.

Illinois Bell's workforce was cut nearly in half, from 26,000 employees to 14,000. By the end of 1982, two-thirds of the study participants were responding very poorly to the stress. Some suffered heart attacks, major depression, and anxiety. Others turned to alcohol and drugs. The marriages of still others fell apart. Some even acted out violently. It was clear that stress was deeply affecting the majority of the study participants.

What's peculiar, however, is that the remaining third of the participants were not only surviving the situation, but thriving in it. It was as though they were living in another reality than their suffering colleagues. Their level of resiliency was much greater than what would be expected under the circumstances. Why was this so?

After poring over the data for months, Sal and his team were able to identify several key attitudes that thriving employees had in common: they viewed their work as worthwhile; they felt they had power to impact the changes happening around them; and they viewed the changes as opportunities for learning and self-improvement. Sal's team saw these three attitudes coming together to produce the personality trait of hardiness.

But interestingly, alongside hardiness, something else arose from the data: those participants who responded positively to the stress practiced *transformational coping*—the notion of imaginatively reframing one's stressful experience, or at least parts of it, into a positive light.

Sal and his research team took a particular interest in one employee, Bill B., who practiced transformational coping in a way that seemed automatic. At fifty-five years of age, Bill managed various aspects of new commercial telephone services for Illinois Bell. As Sal would say, Bill had a "zest for life." In his first interview, the team recognized Bill as unique. He seemed to have all the time in the world, never appearing rushed. The details of the research study interested him. However mundane it was, his work seemed to excite him. He saw his job as playing a small part in helping people connect with one another in ways never before possible.

When asked about the divestiture, Bill displayed no signs of panic or nervousness. He embraced the uncertainty, excited by the evolutionary process in the industry that was happening right in front of him. He knew that whatever his role would be, even if it meant being laid off, he would make the best of it. As the team would note, "Bill looks forward to rolling up his sleeves, working hard, learning new things, and finding silver linings in unexpected places and ways." Throughout the course of the study, Bill exhibited minimal to no mental or physical signs of stress. And, unlike many of his coworkers, he avoided any serious illnesses.

In my research, the ways that I found the playful quality of imagination working in the lives of adults surprised me. I expected to find it used mostly in the context of creative endeavors, such as artistic or musical expression. But instead I found it more frequently being used psychologically, as was the case for the thriving Illinois Bell employees, like Bill, who made their difficult situation more palatable by imaginatively reframing aspects of it. At first glance, the link between imagination and psychological reframing isn't obvious. This is because we don't usually think about imagination as a coping or problem-solving tool. But our imaginations are at play when we are reframing a situation to experience it in a different way. This doesn't, of course, mean that we are trying to escape the situation. It just means that we are trying to think differently about it. In the short term, imaginative reframing helps defuse—but not dismiss—hurt or pain that may have been present from the experience. In the long term, it helps expose growth and learning opportunities.

Like most of us, Bill had learned how to exercise his imagination as a youngster. He had watched his father build furniture and his mother sew extravagant clothing and blankets. Bill had also constructed model airplanes and designed simple comic strips as a child. As an adult, Bill enjoyed using his imagination to build furniture just like his father had done.

While it's helpful to mold our imaginations during childhood, we can just as easily shape and strengthen them in adulthood. The imagination is similar to a muscle needing attention and care: for it to be strong, it must be exercised. Like Bill, what I found to be true in the lives of the playfully intelligent people I interviewed was that spending time exercising one's imagination—by doing things that may seem nonproductive or just plain old fun—makes a big difference when we need to reframe a stressful situation or solve a challenging problem. In other words, activities that exercise the imagination (such as reading fiction, painting, or playing imaginative games) strengthen our imaginations for when we need them most.

●———●

Sheila R.'s mother was young, single, and barely able to care for herself, let alone an unwanted baby. She took Sheila straight from the hospital to her grandmother's house—and walked away. Sheila's grandmother, an eccentric American Indian elder, was also unsuited to raise a child. Married to a hardened New England fisherman, she was ensconced in her own world, a world with no room for a baby. Sheila was frequently left unattended and tied inside her carriage. Her chances of a good life seemed insurmountable.

As a young child, Sheila would strip off her urine-soaked diaper and lie shivering in her carriage until someone finally came to her. She remembers feeling bugs crawling on her while she tried to fall asleep. But she also recalls, even this early in her life, drifting to an imaginary, better world. Playing games in her mind, she was able to find temporary reprieve from her living nightmare.

The state ordered Sheila to live with her mother and two sisters. Still unwanted, Sheila was left in the dank cellar of her mother's friend's house. While living in the cellar, she was bitten on the face by a rat, sending her to the hospital and leaving her scarred from just under her left eye to the bottom of her chin.

Sheila and her sisters were left alone for long stretches of time. One afternoon, the house caught on fire and firefighters scrambled to rescue the three girls, who, having no clean clothes, sat naked in their smoky bedrooms. Sheila's mother ultimately landed in jail for robbery, and the state moved the girls to an orphanage. Then followed the foster-home circuit. One family was wonderful, but the father passed away, and the girls were shipped along. Another family was heartless, verbally and physically abusing Sheila's middle sister for nearly a year. When authorities inquired whether anyone was bothering or hurting them, the terrified girls remained silent, while the perpetrators secretly listened outside the door. When she got older, Sheila became more obstinate and found the courage to write an anonymous letter to the family, saying that the police would soon know about the abuse. When no one confessed to writing the letter, Sheila was sent to the cellar and not allowed out for three days.

Meanwhile, Sheila's imagination got stronger and stronger. While she was living with a city family, she jumped from roof to roof of the tall buildings, pretending that she could fly. While living in the suburbs, she climbed the hills and ventured into the forest. Digging a small hole in the side of the hill, she became a fairy for hours, spinning a magical world around her. Among Sheila and her sisters, she became a fairy princess.

Sheila's third-grade teacher diagnosed Sheila as "illiterate, stupid, and an imbecile," but she actually had dyslexia. Fortunately, Sheila's high school art teacher introduced her to painting, opening a new, creative world for her. Finding solace in painting and drawing, Sheila reflected her peaceful, imaginary world in her art, rather than her dark past. There, she was not just a fairy princess, but also a warrior, a skater, an artist.

Sheila wanted to go to college, something that no one in her family had ever done, but with no money, she instead looked for a husband to support her. She found a man who fit the part and had three daughters within three years. Unfortunately, her husband couldn't hold a job, and unpaid bills stacked up. The stress of life broke their relationship. When a fourth baby, a son whom they would name Bobby, died shortly after birth, the relationship crumbled, and her husband moved out, leaving Sheila and her daughters alone and penniless in a cold-water flat.

Sheila tried to take care of her three daughters with the forty dollars a month she received from welfare. But ultimately she knew she had to make a move. In the late 1960s, at a time when society was rapidly changing, she connected with a group of other mothers and started fighting for mothers' rights. She would speak in front of Congress to plead the needs of the poor; the voice of the warrior had moved from her imagination to her reality.

Sheila's political activism provided more than just a sense of purpose for her: it showed her that despite her tragic life up to that point, she still had a lot of life left to live. She could choose to either go forth with a spirit of positive energy or wallow in regret and self-pity. What emerged was the fairy princess—strong, imaginative, optimistic, and sure. One of her daughters, Dyann, remembers how Sheila wasn't afraid to skip through a parking lot with her or have conversations in made-up languages on buses. No matter how strapped they were for money, Sheila always made allowances for dance classes or small outings that brought her and her daughters joy.

In her thirties, Sheila finally headed to college. But just as her life was beginning to come together, she would meet her greatest challenge so far. At age thirty-five, during her senior year of college, her physician called her to discuss the results of her mammogram. "I have some bad news," he said. Biopsies confirmed breast cancer.

Devastated by the news, Sheila chose to have a relatively new procedure, which at the time had little scientific support: a double mastectomy, followed by breast reconstruction. She would spend two agonizing months in the hospital and then bear multiple rounds of chemotherapy. She thought, "I don't think I can exist. I think I'm going to die. I think I want to die." She asked, "Why am I here? Why did God do this to me?" She had no answers.

After losing plenty of energy to denial, anger, and depression, Sheila regained some of her mental and physical strength and somehow found the fairy princess inside of her again. She decided to finish her college degree. To make up for the time she had lost during her treatments, she took two semesters' worth of classes in one semester. As she saw it, there was no time for worrying about her breast cancer. She would power through on sheer will, and be the best mother she could be.

Sheila completed her degree and, remarkably, graduated with honors. She remembers well that summer after college, enjoying some time off on the Atlantic coast. One particular afternoon, as the sand filled in around her bare feet, Sheila stood surprisingly tall and proud of her surgically reconstructed body. She took a deep breath in and exhaled. Instead of looking at her challenging life and recent cancer diagnosis through a frame of despair, Sheila recognized that remaining angry or frustrated would only hurt her. At that moment, she made a vital commitment: "I'm going to enjoy every last bit of my life."

From then on, Sheila lived her life with a sense of adventure. She spontaneously got into her car and surprised one of her sisters who lived in Maine. She showed up at the airport and took planes to wherever she could. She traveled to Europe. She walked through the cobblestone streets of Spain and saw the Roman relics. She took a cruise with her daughters and spent time with her grandchildren. She learned to ocean kayak. She socialized and made new friends, about whose lives she was eager to learn. Happy to be alive, Sheila had adopted a playful outlook, free from regret about the past or fear of the future.

But again, just as she was getting the spring back in her step, Sheila, now in her early sixties, started to feel intermittent, nagging pains in her body. Her primary care physician ordered an x-ray. It showed a concerning area in the bone of her left shoulder. A CAT scan revealed multiple abnormal areas throughout her skeleton—in her chest bone, hip, spine, the long bones of her arm, and all over her skull. A biopsy confirmed metastatic breast cancer.

As they received the news, Sheila and her daughters sat motionless in the office of Dr. Kellie Sprague, Sheila's oncologist. How much time did Sheila have? Reluctant to offer false hope, Dr. Sprague told Sheila and her family that some people lived for up to five years. Her daughters turned to Sheila, expecting tears. But Sheila simply began making a list of all the things she still wanted to do: paint, write, and travel. Live, give, and love. Share. Teach. Sheila also wanted to pass on to her family an important lesson that she had learned in her life: "Try to let things go more easily, and live lighter than you are. You end up hurting yourself if you don't."

Refusing to let metastatic breast cancer get her down, Sheila started hormone and radiation therapy to slow down her disease and ease her pain. In year five, an MRI of her brain suggested that there was breast cancer in her brain tissue. Gamma knife surgery, which delivers targeted doses of radiation to cancer cells, was recommended. Most people who undergo gamma knife surgery are terrified. But Sheila is not most people. When she came out of the surgery, she was beaming (pun intended) about how the radiation oncologist could activate certain areas of her brain to make her fingers and toes move. Her daughter said to her, "Mom! That was *not* you laughing in there, was it?"

Over the past several years, Sheila has encountered other bumps in the road, including a stroke and a recent hysterectomy for breast cancer in her uterus. But somehow she has been able to maintain her playful countenance. Now in her seventies, Sheila sometimes aggravates her children with her spontaneous antics and insatiable desire for excitement and adventure. "No, Mom, you can't learn to skydive at your age!" Sometimes she listens, depending on how much her desire burns (she hasn't taken up skydiving), and sometimes she doesn't. Her daughters compare her to a four-year-old riding in a car, with her cheerful remarks: "Oh, my goodness, look at that mailbox! Have they changed the shape of mailboxes?" "A red sweater! You'd look great in a red sweater!"

Sheila's ability to be playful at all is miraculous. Behind her seasoned smile and soft, crystal-blue eyes, one might expect a hint of melancholy smoldering in the remains of anger and frustration. But it simply isn't there. From her horrific childhood to her life now, enduring metastatic breast cancer for twelve years, Sheila has imaginatively reframed her entire existence.

Perhaps no one knows better how unusual Sheila is than Dr. Sprague. When asked about her, Dr. Sprague noted how rare it was for someone to have such a late recurrence of cancer, twenty-four years after the diagnosis. And to live over ten years with bony metastasis is not unheard of, but extremely uncommon. Dr. Sprague has seen what usually happens when someone's cancer progresses after being stable. The shock factor often shreds any hope that had built up. Sheila, however, accepted each new recurrence and complication in stride. Here's how Dr. Sprague describes it:

> Sheila has definitely reframed her life. I can't prove this by science, but I feel attitude does matter. Sheila is an extremely playful person. She's very lighthearted . . . not a "Debbie Downer." She's very involved with her kids and grandkids, holidays, birthdays, and weddings. She doesn't miss out. Her creativity is her outlet. She's even made me hats and scarves. These are happy things for her. She's not in denial. [The cancer] is very much a part of her life.
>
> Doctors have to be careful to not make people feel like they're not doing well if they aren't

happy-go-lucky. But I do feel strongly that those who have a good attitude, people that can be positive—and they can't be positive all the time, but if they live more of the time in that positive spirit, their experience is better. It may not change their cancer, but it changes their experience, how they live with it. The patients who have these positive attitudes still die from their cancer, but they have a much better experience. Sheila is the epitome of this person.

When I tell other patients it is possible to live a long time, it's true. I can speak the truth because Sheila has done it and has shown me that it can be done well. She is living from her cancer, rather than dying from it.

Sheila, like Bill and the other Illinois Bell employees who used the playful quality of imagination to reframe their experiences, knows that stress is unavoidable and that managing it, in part by imaginative reframing, is a much more fulfilling way to live than trying to run away from it altogether.

Life continues to offer Sheila one challenge after the next. And while she now recognizes that there are so many things she can't do, she focuses on the many things she *can* do. Adept at using her imagination to reframe, Sheila sprinkles a little of her fairy dust around her and makes her world, and everyone in it, better. Sheila's daughter Dyann says it best:

I think that my mom was put here to add a little sunshine from dark corners. She's one of the strongest women I know. She always has a smile on her face, trying to find the shiny penny. She uses her imagination to get around things, through things, and over things. Her imagining things to be better actually *makes* them better.

●━━━●

Understanding the neuroscience of imaginative reframing helps explain why it's so powerful. When you use your imagination to reframe situations, the left lateral, prefrontal cortex in your brain is activated. This region acts like a mental sketchpad, representing information not currently in your environment. When the sketchpad is opened, activity in other areas of your brain—specifically the ones that control emotions—dampens. This allows you to thrive in stressful experiences and not succumb to the challenging emotions that may arise.

At the neuronal level, when your imagination is reframing, Hebb's Law of neuroscience is being disturbed—which is a good thing. The law says: neurons that fire together, wire together. This means that if you always use the same tricks to solve problems, or always assess situations through the same worn-out, customary frames, those connections in your brain become rigid. In other words, if you continue to react to difficult situations with fear, then difficult situations will always wire with fear-based emotions in your brain. Imaginative reframing disturbs and helps unsync this.

Alex Osborn's 1953 book, *Applied Imagination*, pioneered the idea of "brainstorming," which good imaginative reframing incorporates to a large extent. Osborn described two principles that are essential for high-quality brainstorming: 1) deferment of judgment and 2) quantity over quality. These same principles apply to imaginative reframing. When we are trying to reframe a difficult situation in our lives, it's important not to criticize any of the frames that our imaginations are drawing on our mental sketchpads. Criticism and judgment will strengthen the fear-based emotions that we are trying to gently reduce with more resourceful reframings. They will also limit the number of frames that we can produce, causing us to fall back on old wiring.

Anette Prehn, a sociologist and keynote speaker who studies the science of reframing, has developed a model called "Framestorm," to help apply reframing techniques to everyday life. To become a better reframer, whenever one spots old frames intertwined with unhealthy emotions, Anette advocates initiating a Framestorm to disrupt the old neural connections and forge new ones.

Like Osborn's brainstorming, the key to Framestorming is to "just keep going," no matter how outlandish the frames are that your imagination is creating. Anette puts it well: "When the reframing brainstorm begins, the individual gently and playfully pauses the neural connection that has always fired and redirects attention to constructive alternatives that induce resourcefulness." In other words, a Framestorm is not just about thinking outside the box. It's about creating a whole new box altogether. And then creating another, and another, and another.

Anette also notes that Framestorming, like brainstorming, advocates deferring judgment—but only temporarily. Eventually, one must draw upon his or her judgment when choosing which reframings to give special attention to.

One example illustrating Framestorming that Anette shares is the story of Kevin T., a branch manager at a bank. Kevin found himself becoming very frightened by the thought of someone robbing his bank, especially after his wife, who also worked in banking, experienced a robbery herself. Kevin's intense fear put him on the verge of switching careers. So Anette walked Kevin through a robbery Framestorm.

It began with Kevin reframing a robbery not only as a threat, but also as an opportunity to support others, tune in to life's priorities, and remember life's fragility. It then progressed to realizing that, from a pure statistical standpoint, a robbery normally ends with the employees going home to their families again. Kevin also saw robbery through the frame of how it might strengthen his empathy for others who have gone through traumatic experiences. This led him to the point of recognizing robbery as a desperate person's (false) hope of a better life. He let his imagination loose and thought metaphorically about robbery as an earthquake, saying, "Robbery shakes you, but the earth doesn't have to crack. Unexpected situations can arise anywhere, anytime."

After his Framestorm, Kevin became calmer about the prospect of robbery at his bank. He also told Anette that imaginatively reframing something as extreme as robbery had even boosted his ability to use reframing in his life on a more general level.

Another way to look at the neuroscience of reframing

is through psychologist Abraham Luchins's classic 1942 experiment called "The Water Jar Test." Study subjects were separated into two groups. Each group was given the same three jars (A, B, and C), each with a capacity to hold a different, fixed amount of water. Luchins then gave both groups a fourth jar (D) and asked them to fill it with specified amounts of water. The first five amounts that were assigned to Group 1 for Jar D only had one solution: Jar B – Jar A – Jar C – Jar C. For example, say that Jar A was capable of holding 21 units of water, Jar B 127 units, and Jar C 3 units. To fill Jar D with 100 units, the only solution would be to fill Jar B completely with water and then pour out enough water to fill Jar A once and Jar C twice (127 – 21 – 3 – 3 = 100). The effect of solving assigned amounts that only had one solution was that Group 1 became subconsciously biased toward using only the B – A – 2C solution. Conversely, Group 2 was assigned water amounts that had multiple solutions, and thus they didn't become biased toward using the B – A – 2C solution. So, when subjects in Group 1 were assigned 18 units of water from jars with capacities 15, 39, and 3, they used the more cumbersome B – A – 2C (39 – 15 – 3 – 3 = 18) solution that they were biased toward, whereas Group 2 opted for the simpler, more efficient solution of A + C (15 + 3 = 18).

Luchins termed this phenomenon the "Einstellung Effect." *Einstellung* means "setting" or "installation" in German. The Einstellung Effect is the development of a mechanized state of mind, referring to a predisposition to solve a problem based on previous experience, even though a better way to solve the problem exists.

Einstellung is essentially the negative effect, or influence, of previous experience when solving new problems.

If we rely too much on our past experiences to solve a problem, we allow the brain's connections that have always fired together to continue firing (and wiring!) together. This is how we get stuck. But when we exercise our imaginations to reframe a problem, we open our minds, and our wiring, to a new way of looking at the world. It's almost as if we're inviting the body's processes to work a little differently, helping us to function better and grow and learn from our stressors.

As we will see next, there's another psychological phenomenon, besides reframing, that the playful quality of imagination also bolsters—and it rests at the crux of how we come to understand each other.

●———●

Constantly overshadowed by his overachieving older brother, John F. Kennedy, "Jack" for short, quickly established a distinctive personality that helped him stand out in his Irish-Catholic family: he would be the clown. Once, he stole a cardboard cutout of Mae West from the cinema and left it in his bed to shock the family's housemaid. Another time, he exploded a toilet seat with a firecracker. Breaking the rules, coming late to dinner, dressing messily, and asking inappropriate questions during religious instruction were signature moves.

Besides Kennedy being different and more fun than his serious older brother, his joie de vivre may have also evolved in part from his lifelong battle with chronic illnesses. Though kept private, with many details still unknown to this day, Kennedy was sick from age thirteen on. His first diagnosis was "colitis" of unclear cause. By his twenties, he had chronic back pain, eventually undergoing several spinal surgeries. In his thirties, as a congressman, he was diagnosed with Addison's disease, a rare endocrine disorder leading to adrenal gland failure. After being told that he might soon die from Addison's, Kennedy made the decision to treat each day as if it were his last, demanding adventure and excitement from his life.

During his presidency from 1961 to 1963, JFK fostered an unconventional style of running the Oval Office. Rather than emphasizing the ceremonial aspects of meetings, such as photo ops and handshakes, he focused on people and their personalities, favoring more personal, informal meetings. His unusual, "ordinary" wit, charm, and humor put people at ease and made him fun to work with.

Kennedy first met his Cuban Missile Crisis counterpart, Soviet premier Nikita Khrushchev, during one of Khrushchev's visits to Camp David in 1959. Kennedy had been one of twenty-five senators willing to meet with "one of the biggest communists on the planet." Though they met only briefly, Khrushchev would later remark that Kennedy's "good-natured smile" left a favorable impression on him.

In June of 1961, the two again met face-to-face at the Vienna Summit. The summit had been designed to provide an open forum for discussion about the Cold War, with the hope of improving relations between the two superpowers.

In preparation for Vienna, Kennedy had spent a

tremendous amount of time reviewing previous correspondence with Khrushchev, even interviewing those
who knew him personally. He had studied Khrushchev's
personality, trying to imagine what it would be like to be
him. Just before the summit, veteran diplomat Averell
Harriman offered some advice to Kennedy:

> Go to Vienna and don't be too serious—have some
> fun, get to know him a little, don't let him rattle
> you . . . . His style will be to attack and then see if
> he can get away with it. Laugh about it. Don't get
> into a fight. Rise above it. Have some fun.

Kennedy must have heeded this advice, for Khrushchev again found him to be pleasant, reasonable, and
easy to joke with. At one point, Kennedy raised a glass
to Khrushchev, expressing admiration for his vigor and
energy as well as hope for a better understanding between their two nations. Khrushchev expressed similar
optimisms, and throughout the meeting, the two were able
to relax and laugh together despite the backdrop of the
Cold War.

Notwithstanding the pleasantries, Kennedy thought
Khrushchev was particularly tough, yet he understood
Khrushchev's need to appease his military and allies.
Khrushchev found that Kennedy drew an equally hard
line, but he liked his frankness and sense of humor.
Khrushchev also recognized the effect of his toughness
on Kennedy. At a reception in a theater during their last
night, Kennedy's facial expression conveyed anxiety and
disappointment. Khrushchev knew that they would be
unable to reach an agreement. He said:

Politics is a merciless business, but that realization didn't keep me from feeling sorry for Kennedy. As one human being to another, I felt bad about his disappointment. . . . I knew his enemies, especially aggressive politicians, would take advantage of him and tease him, saying, "See? They tricked you; they gave your nose a good pull." That's what I imagined the president expected to hear when he got home. I felt doubly sorry because what happened did not create favorable conditions for improving relations.

Vienna ended with no tangible solutions to the Cold War tensions. But it did lay the groundwork for a relationship between Kennedy and Khrushchev, which continued to grow through acts of goodwill. This included a special gift from Khrushchev to Jacqueline Kennedy—a dog named Pushinka, whose mother was Strelka, the first dog sent into space by the Soviet Union. After undergoing a battery of tests to search for hidden listening devices, microphones, bombs, and germs, Pushinka was finally allowed into the White House. In a letter to Khrushchev, Kennedy joked, "Her flight from the Soviet Union to the United States was not as dramatic as the flight of her mother, nevertheless, it was a long voyage and she stood it well."

On October 14, 1962, an American spy plane photographed the Soviet Union's building of nuclear-missile bases in Cuba. The Soviets were responding to both the Bay of Pigs Invasion, a failed expatriate coup attempt on Cuba sponsored by the Central Intelligence Agency, and the United States' escalation of its nuclear presence in Turkey, whose warheads could easily reach Moscow. If the Soviets activated their nuclear weapons in Cuba, between 80 and 100 million Americans would die. If the United States preempted the strike, over 100 million Russians would die. To give these numbers perspective, in World War II, which included the only two nuclear bombs ever used in warfare, over 60 million people were killed in six years. An American–Soviet nuclear war would double that toll in a matter of minutes. The Cuban Missile Crisis was the pinnacle of Cold War tension and fear.

In the first days of the Cuban Missile Crisis, Kennedy knew that Khrushchev wanted peace as much as he did, and he recognized that no matter what course of action was pursued, he needed to give Khrushchev time to respond. Otherwise, Khrushchev might carelessly act on his emotions. Going against his advisers, who encouraged a massive air strike on Cuba, Kennedy opted to quarantine the island country with a ring of ships, cutting off military supplies being delivered to Cuba from the Soviet Union.

What ensued over the next several days was a series of remarkable personal correspondences, via letter exchanges, between the two leaders. In the letters, both Kennedy and Khrushchev acknowledged the other's position, including the stress and terrible responsibility imposed on someone holding the key to nuclear weapons. Eventually, Khrushchev proposed a solution to the dilemma: if the United States would end the quarantine, give its word that it would not invade Cuba, and remove its warheads from Turkey, the Soviet Union would remove its presence from Cuba. After intense deliberation by Kennedy and his advisers, the United States agreed. On October 28, 1962, the Cuban Missile Crisis officially ended. Robert S. McNamara, Kennedy's Secretary of Defense, would later publicly remark that empathy had played a central role in the resolution of the Cuban Missile Crisis. Perhaps the hardest thing to imagine is empathizing with an enemy, as was the case between Kennedy and Khrushchev. Kennedy's playful nature worked in his favor when it came time to imagine what Khrushchev was thinking and feeling during the crisis. Khrushchev was certainly a more serious personality than Kennedy, but he too was spontaneous and had a sense of humor.

In our own lives, people cross our paths who play the role of our temporary (and sometimes not-so-temporary) enemies: the driver who cuts us off when we're already late; guests who point out the one thing wrong with the gourmet dinner that took us three hours to prepare; a coworker who keeps rubbing us the wrong way; our child who has a fit because their TV time is over. Empathizing with these "enemies" may seem inopportune at the time, but it may be exactly what's needed to resolve the conflict at hand.

●——●

Empathy is one of the most powerful tools we have for establishing, building, deepening, and maintaining healthy relationships. Though imagination is not the first thing that comes to mind when we consider empathizing with another person, it is actually the seed of empathy. When we use our imagination to put ourselves in someone else's shoes, we are better able to understand his or her situation and establish deeper connections.

This is the other theme that, like reframing, repeated itself over and over in my interviews and observations of playfully intelligent people. The playful quality of imagination helps us attain an empathic state of mind. Consider for a moment what would happen if, during an interaction with someone, you were perpetually asking yourself, "How does this person feel right now? Where, exactly, is he or she mentally and emotionally?" Your imagination would be on fire! You'd also be exhausted and probably wouldn't have the greatest interaction. But taking just a few seconds to imagine yourself in another's shoes, both before and during an interaction, can help set the tone for a mutually beneficial experience.

So, if the playful quality of imagination is the workhorse of reframing and empathy, the big question is whether there is evidence showing that exercising the imagination, as if it were a muscle, prepares it for when one needs to reframe or empathize.

In 1977, Susan J. Frank, a young psychologist at the University of Maryland, looked into this exact question. She noticed that some of her clients who exercised their imaginations through daydreaming seemed to have a deeper empathetic understanding of people. An avid daydreamer herself, she designed a research study to determine whether daydreaming was associated with increased empathetic abilities. What she found confirmed her hypothesis: people could, in fact, exercise their imaginations through daydreaming and, in turn, increase their capacity for empathy.

One example in Frank's study involved a black student from the South who was struggling to fit into a predominantly white, Ivy League culture. Frank gave her students a daydreaming exercise in which she asked the students to imagine that they were alone in a crowd of people. The black student envisioned himself at a college party, sitting on a luggage trunk in a corner. In this scenario, he imagined a white student at the party whom he perceived as a "snob who could never consider talking to a black Southern peon like himself." But then, because of his previous exposure to daydreaming exercises, he shifted his contemplation to imagine being in the white student's shoes. He viewed the white student's perspective of himself as a snob, too taken with himself to join the group, someone who probably "hated white people, anyway."

The other participants listened to the black student describe his daydream. When he opened his eyes, he saw looks of surprise on their faces. Indeed, they had thought that he was too taken with himself to become a part of the group. As the study progressed, the black student became a leader in the group, helping other students express their feelings more openly and understand other people's perceptions without judgment.

Reading fiction is another way one can exercise the imagination to strengthen empathy. Raymond Mar, a social psychologist at York University in Toronto, Canada, has studied how fiction readers are more empathetic. In one of his studies, which he aptly titled "Bookworms versus Nerds," he found that readers of fiction have stronger senses of empathy than readers of nonfiction. This effect could not be attributed to age, experience with English, or general intelligence. Mar concluded that "bookworms," by reading a great deal of fiction, likely buffer themselves from the effects of reduced interpersonal contact by simulating the social experiences depicted in the stories they are reading. On the other hand, "nerds" who read nonfiction almost exclusively don't simulate the social experiences and thus may not derive the social skills that the real world requires. (If you are, in fact, a "nerd" reading this book, I do encourage you to continue reading, but perhaps consider adding some fiction to your nightstand!)

In his book *Applied Imagination*, Alex Osborn also supports the imagination-muscle metaphor. He suggests traveling as another way to exercise imagination. It needn't be to someplace exotic; it can be within your own town. But it should be an "out-of-the-way" place, and the experience should be approached in a "rough-it-as-you-go" manner. He also suggests quick and easy exercises, such as cutting out cartoons or comics, omitting the original captions, and rewriting the stories. Or, in less than a hundred words, writing an outline of an original story for children.

All in all, it makes sense that when the imagination is exercised, it is strengthened for situations down the road, like when we need to reframe misfortune into opportunity or empathize with a friend or foe. And when we become more aware of the unexpected benefits of an active imagination, we begin to see it—and ourselves—in a different, new light.

⊷

The parent lottery had not been kind to Josie. Her mother and father were both alcoholics, and she began to follow suit at age fifteen. Josie's addiction started with a beer here and there. Then came vodka. By her senior year of high school, she was drinking nearly every day.

Somehow, Josie graduated and left the house. She found a one-bedroom apartment in the next town over and worked at different clothing stores. She would make it about a year at each store. Usually, either being late or the smell of alcohol on her breath got her fired. Josie was good at her job. She loved fashion and helping people find just the right pieces of clothing.

In her late twenties, Josie met a man at a dance club. They hit it off. He worked in construction. He drank, too, but not nearly as much as her. The two got married and had a daughter named Alicia. The first two years of Alicia's life were some of Josie's best years. She was drinking less and holding down a job. Her marriage seemed to be working.

But as Josie approached her mid-thirties, her drinking picked up again. She sought help through Alcoholics Anonymous, but couldn't kick the disease. Her friendships started to vanish, and her husband filed for divorce and got full custody of Alicia. The court ordered Josie to undergo intensive alcohol rehabilitation, but allowed her to have periodic visitations with Alicia.

Rehab worked a little bit, but Josie always relapsed. Her drinking was now regularly landing her in the hospital. Her liver had been damaged by the years of alcohol abuse, and her pancreas often became acutely inflamed, causing her excruciating upper abdominal pain. She would sometimes have to stay in the hospital for a week or more, eating very little, until her pancreas cooled down.

By age thirty-seven, Josie had essentially lost everything—except her booze.

By contrast, the parent lottery had been kind to Megan, who, like Josie, had grown up in a small town. Megan's mother and father weren't alcoholics; they were hardworking and loving, and they did everything possible to mold Megan into a responsible, productive, and happy adult. They weren't perfect, and they were careful not to make things too easy for Megan. But they were always there for her when she needed to fall into their arms after an academic disappointment, a loss in sports, or a fizzled romance.

Megan wasn't great on standardized tests, but she made up for it with a tenacious work ethic that helped her earn good grades in high school. Well-respected by her classmates, Megan graduated with honors and attended college at an elite university on the East Coast. She majored in biology and loved science.

Megan decided that she wanted to become a physician and applied to twenty medical schools across the country. She was admitted to a handful of them and settled on one that was near her undergraduate institution. Megan saw medicine as an opportunity to help others, while pursuing her love of science.

Academically, Megan was an above-average medical student, but she rose to the top of her class when it came to bedside manner. She always warmly connected with her patients and made them feel heard and cared for. One of Megan's mentors once described her approach as "effortless and natural."

After medical school, Megan pursued residency in internal medicine. She thought being an internist would allow her to develop lasting relationships with her patients and also put her bedside talents to use. But despite the strong foundation that Megan's parents had provided for her and her success in medical school, Megan struggled in residency. It was much harder than she had expected, and she was deeply affected by it: the awfully sick patients whom she couldn't help; the patients who were hurting themselves with tobacco, alcohol, and overeating; the long hours in the hospital; and the lack of time for nurturing personal interests outside of medicine. She also felt like an inexperienced chef in the hospital wards, following treatment recipes that left very little room, if any, for imagination and the art of medicine.

Although she was not entirely conscious of it at the time, toward the end of her residency, Megan's capacity for being present with her patients had greatly waned. Her residency training had made her proficient in the diagnosis and treatment of disease, but paradoxically deficient in the empathy and benevolence of healing. Megan hoped that her spark for medicine would return once she started practicing.

Megan's last night on call as a resident took place in late June. She and the intern she was supervising had just finished eating dinner together. They were preparing to run their list of patients, which is when the intern and his or her senior resident discuss the management and treatment plans for the patients who have been admitted. After the list is run, the senior resident circles around to the rooms of the patients that he or she has not yet seen. These patients are usually clinically stable, as the senior resident sees the unstable patients right away with the intern.

It had been a slower call night. Megan and her intern had only four admissions, two of whom Megan needed to meet. The first was an older man who had fallen at home earlier in the day. There was a question of whether he had fainted or tripped over a rug in his house. His laboratory and cardiac tests were reassuring. Megan entered his room. He was sitting up in bed, having dinner, and watching baseball on television. She introduced herself briefly and then told him the plan for the evening. It was a short visit.

Megan then headed toward the stairwell. The second patient's room was one floor up. As she climbed the stairs, Megan read the notes she had taken when she and her intern had run the list:

Female, 37. Alcohol abuse since 15. Early cirrhosis, admitted with upper abdominal pain. Labs c/w acute alcoholic pancreatitis. Multiple admissions for same. Actively drinking. Divorced. One daughter. Fluids, pain control.

Name—Josie.

Megan knocked on the door and stepped into Josie's room.

"I'm your senior resident this evening. My name is Megan. I think you've met my intern."

"Hello, I'm Josie. Yes, she said you'd be coming by."

Megan sat in a chair next to Josie's bed. She anticipated another short visit and was looking forward to heading back to her call room.

"How's your pain?" Megan asked.

"Still there, but not as bad as this morning," Josie said.

"You've been drinking since you were in high school?"

"Yup."

"You know alcohol is killing your liver and pancreas, right?"

"I know."

"You've really got to stop drinking," Megan said emphatically.

Josie looked down at her hands. "Yeah, that's what they tell me."

Megan gazed out the window. She didn't have the energy to meet Josie where she was, nor could she envision what Josie's life might be like. She faulted Josie for drinking, which allowed her to mentally avoid connecting with her.

Megan stood up and prepared to leave Josie's room. Suddenly, she heard a young girl's voice coming from the door.

"Mommy! Mommy!"

Megan turned around. There, standing in the doorway, was an adorable eight-year-old girl with light brown hair and hazel eyes. She was smiling and holding a piece of paper.

"Are you my mommy's doctor?" the girl asked.

Clearing her throat, Megan replied, "Uh, yes . . . yes, I'm one of them."

"I'm Alicia," the girl said. She waved at Megan, and Megan waved back.

"Is that really *you*, Alicia?" Josie exclaimed.

"Yes, it's me!" Alicia ran to Josie, climbed into her bed, and gave her a big hug.

"Did Daddy bring you here?" Josie asked.

"Yes, he's across the hall in the waiting room."

"Tell him thank you from me, okay?"

Alicia handed a piece of paper to Josie. Josie's eyes began to water.

"That's you, Mommy, in the middle. You're in a storm, but see . . ."

Alicia pointed to the upper right corner of the picture.

"There's some sunshine peeking out from the clouds. You'll get through this, Mommy."

Alicia had drawn her picture with colored pencils. Josie was in the middle of the page, surrounded by black and gray clouds. The only color on the page was a wisp of yellow in the upper right-hand corner and some green, pink, and purple on the dress that Alicia had drawn on Josie (Alicia knew her mom liked fashion). Josie blotted her tears from her eyes with her finger, and she and Alicia snuggled and continued to chat.

Megan slid quietly out of the room and walked back to her call room. When she got there, she closed the door behind her and took a deep breath. This was her last night on call. She sat on the edge of the bed and looked down at the ground. One would expect Megan to feel happy and relieved since it was her last night, but she didn't. She couldn't stop thinking about Alicia's picture. With it, Alicia had done everything that Megan had failed to do. Alicia had drawn Josie alone, surrounded by a thunderstorm. This was how Alicia saw Josie: as someone who was alone, and maybe lonely, too. And as someone who was scared—the kind of scared that amounted to a thunderstorm in an eight-year-old's mind. The sun was Alicia's sign of hope. She wanted Josie (and probably herself) to believe that better days were ahead. Using her imagination, Alicia understood how her mom was feeling and had offered her some hope.

Empathy through imagination, plus a little bit of hope—medicine doesn't get much simpler than that, Megan thought.

She quickly gathered a few things in her call room and walked back to Josie's room. Josie was still awake; Alicia and her dad had just left. Megan knocked on the door.

"Come in," said Josie. She looked up and saw the serious expression on Megan's face. "Is everything okay?" Josie asked.

"Yes, everything's fine," Megan said. "Well, kind of. I'm back because . . . because I never said goodbye. And I never really said hello, either. I'd like to learn more about your story, if you'll share it with me."

Josie was excited that someone actually wanted to listen to her story without judgment. Over the next hour, they talked about Josie's life. Once they had finished, Megan—much to her surprise—caught an hour or so of sleep on Josie's floor.

When Megan's pager went off in the early morning hours, Josie stirred a little, but didn't wake up. Megan calmly collected her things. As she was leaving the room, she noticed a framed photo of Alicia on Josie's nightstand.

"Thank you, Alicia," she whispered. With Josie sleeping peacefully, Megan quietly left the room.

Imagination Well Played

Reframe Readiness

Here are a few tips to help you exercise your imagination's reframing capacity:

• **Notice your thoughts, nonjudgmentally.** This is a good habit to have, whether you are reframing or not. Take a moment to notice your thoughts, observing them as they pass like clouds in the sky. Do certain thoughts tend to recur or stick around? Think about your thoughts objectively, without labels or criticism. Then try to detach any emotion tied to them. A good way to do this is to say the emotions out loud. Hearing the words that describe your emotions will help train your brain to separate your thoughts from your emotions when you are trying to use your imagination to reframe.

• **Examine your stressor.** Sometimes, even after you've untwisted your thoughts from your emotions, your thoughts might still feel like a group of racing thoroughbreds, thundering down the final stretch. This usually happens when you are dealing with a lot of stress and trying to manage it too quickly. You might fail to think about what is (or isn't) actually happening. Is there validity to the perceived stress? Is there an underlying misunderstanding? Is something truly being threatened? Can something actually be changed about the situation? Asking these types of questions will help bring the horses of thought back to the starting gate.

- **Choose your own adventure.** The next time you are faced with a situation or experience that you would like to try to reframe, pretend that you are writing a *Choose Your Own Adventure* novel. First, imagine two ways in which the scenario could be worse and elaborate on the worse of the two inside your mind. Then imagine two ways in which it could be better and spin a tad more intricate tale about the better scenario. Try to incorporate humor into your stories. Try to also find a few blessings in disguise and a few thorns on the rosebush in both the bad and good stories you have created. By doing this, you will be reminded that everything has pros and cons, which will help keep your emotions in check when you are reframing.

Empathize with Your Enemy

Imagining yourself in the shoes of someone you're in conflict with may seem like the last thing you want to do. But empathizing with the "enemy" may be the key to resolving the issues at hand.

The first step is to really imagine being the other person. Consider his or her particular situation. What drives that person's emotions? Mirror the person as accurately as possible: assume his or her body position, posture, tone, gestures, and facial expressions. How do you view yourself through that person's eyes?

The next step is to become aware of three pitfalls that you may face:

1. **Overlooking your enemy's longing for peace.** It can be easy to forget that your enemy ultimately wants the same thing that you want—peace. As that person, ask yourself, "What do I really want from life?" Chances are that you will come up with answers similar to your own, such as safety, security, and love. These basic human needs often drive the fear leading to conflict. Sometimes the recognition of someone's desire for peace is enough to defuse tension.

2. **Overlooking your enemy's fear of being attacked.** When under attack, whether psychologically or physically, people get defensive. Lashing out can seem like the only choice. As your enemy, ask yourself, "What am I afraid of?" Are you afraid of being attacked? While in that person's shoes, look at yourself as the attacker. What stance are you taking that poses a threat to your foe?

3. **Overlooking your enemy's understandable anger.** Still at your boiling point? Try standing in your opponent's shoes and feeling that person's anger. This one works particularly well with family members or friends. Often someone sees only his or her own side of the argument. While imagining yourself as your enemy, ask yourself why you are so angry.

What a Day for a Daydream

Having been scolded for zoning out during high school chemistry, you might still tell yourself that wandering thoughts are a waste of time. But besides helping develop empathy, daydreaming also improves memory, consolidates learning, and promotes creativity. To optimize the power of your daydreaming, you first need to be aware that daydreams, and the thoughts contained in them, can be negative just as often as they can be positive. To tilt your balance in a positive direction, try the following:

• **Reframe daydreaming.** Give yourself permission to let your mind wander. Take a moment to absolve yourself of any guilt associated with daydreaming. Recognize that you are doing something good for yourself.

• **Timing is everything.** When practicing, choose a time when you can put your responsibilities on hold for a few minutes. Early morning or just before you fall asleep might be when your mind is most relaxed and there are the fewest distractions.

• **Focus first.** Similar to tightening a muscle before allowing it to relax, it is helpful to focus your mind on something before allowing it to wander. Try focusing on your breathing for five breaths. You can focus on the sensation of your breath within your body. Or you can focus on the words *in* and *out*.

• **Select a subject.** The subject of your daydream matters. Some subjects won't be productive (for example, romantic partners that you don't currently or will never have). Daydreaming instead about an existing or a potentially realistic relationship will translate into better results. Try dreaming about an adventure or expedition that you've always wanted to experience.

Sweet daydreams!

CHAPTER TWO

Sociability

B orn on March 26, 1975, to a tenth-generation white sharecropping family, Percy Strickland lived with his mother, father, and older brother on a diversified crop farm in the poor, rural town of Spivey's Corner, North Carolina. They raised hogs and various crops, and dinner was always on the table, but sharecropping didn't cover all the expenses. Everyone had side jobs to make ends meet.

As Percy grew older, his responsibilities on the farm also grew. He spent a lot of time working with his grandfather, Luke Strickland. One of the most sociable people in Spivey's Corner, Grandpa Luke never met a stranger— just a friend he didn't know yet. Percy and his grandfather chopped cotton together in the field. After the work was done, they would drive to the country store. Percy always rode in the bed of Grandpa Luke's pickup truck. With his bright blond hair, white t-shirt, and denim overalls, Percy would lean over the edge of the truck, smiling widely as he watched the fields pass by.

The bed of the truck was Percy's spot because Grandpa Luke had a habit of giving a ride to those in need. Many found comfort in Grandpa Luke's passenger seat. He always saw his riders as people who might need a listening ear or to simply be seen from the inside, rather than the outside.

Being raised on a farm, Percy learned the value of hard work at a young age. School didn't necessarily come easy for him, but his above-average intelligence, combined with a strong work ethic, helped him earn admission to Duke University. He would be the first person in his family to attend college.

Duke was a culture shock for Percy, to put it mildly. Most Duke students aren't raised on hog farms, surrounded by poverty. The majority hail from middle- to upper-class families. On freshman move-in day, Percy showed up at his dorm and began to unload his belongings. His dad, wearing a dark-blue work uniform, followed behind him, carrying under just one arm the mini-fridge that Percy had received as a high school graduation present. As the two transferred Percy's things to his room, a father of another incoming freshman said to Percy, "The university staff is so amazingly helpful. I could never have carried that mini-fridge!"

Fortunately, Percy found a sense of belonging amid Duke's InterVarsity Christian Fellowship group, and rather than hiding his background or trying to be someone he wasn't, Percy reached back to the important lessons he had learned in Spivey's Corner. He kept at his coursework with the same diligence that he had applied to his farm work. And like his Grandpa Luke, he saw others as passengers in the pickup truck that was his own life, treating everyone equally and showing them a sense of humility that was aligned with his humble beginnings. Each of his social interactions were seen as an opportunity to brighten someone else's day and form a connection. His friends saw him as someone who didn't take himself too seriously, but who cared about them deeply. With a self-deprecating sense of humor and a playful goofiness, Percy began building lifelong relationships.

After graduation, Percy married his college sweetheart, Angie. The two moved to Richmond, Virginia, so that Angie could attend medical school at Virginia Commonwealth University. Not knowing exactly what his career path would be, Percy joined the staff of the University of Richmond's InterVarsity group. He knew that the group would put his skills to use, at least temporarily, while Angie started medical school. But what came as a surprise to him was how much an interaction he would have with a University of Richmond student would change the trajectory of his life.

Andy, an undergraduate, came to Percy because he was feeling uncomfortable at the University of Richmond. He was having trouble developing friendships and, being passionate about his religion, wanted to transfer to a bible college, where he could work toward becoming an overseas missionary. Percy wondered how Andy would be successful in overseas missions work—a mostly social endeavor—when he was finding it hard to connect with the folks around him.

Percy decided to study the biblical parable of the Good Samaritan with Andy. In the popular parable, an expert in law asks Jesus what he must do to inherit eternal life. Jesus instructs him to love God completely and love his neighbor as himself, to which the expert responds, "And who is my neighbor?" Jesus answers the expert by telling the story of a Jewish man who has been brutally attacked by robbers and left for dead. Three other men, a priest, a Levite, and a Samaritan, encounter the injured man, in that order. The first two men, for one reason or another, don't stop. But the Samaritan, who represents the great divide between Jews and Samaritans, unexpectedly stops and helps the man. Jesus then asks the expert who the neighbor is in the story, and the expert correctly answers that it's the Samaritan.

Percy thought the parable might inspire Andy to connect more locally with other students, especially those who might, at first glance, seem different than him. Essentially, he wanted Andy to become a better neighbor within his world of Richmond, Virginia. But Andy came back with a question for Percy: "What are your neighbors like?"

Andy wasn't trying to be confrontational. He figured that Percy had developed relationships with his neighbors. But Percy hadn't. He and Angie were living in a large apartment complex in a nice part of Richmond, and they really hadn't gotten to know any of their neighbors yet.

The next day, Percy began randomly knocking on his neighbors' doors to introduce himself. People thought he was a salesman. Percy recalls a lot of laughing and looks on people's faces that said, "Are you serious?" as he explained to each perplexed person, in his own humble way, that he was simply trying to get to know his neighbors better.

Andy's question kept lingering in Percy's mind for the next several weeks. Percy had an amazing gift for playful sociability, but he had lost sight of what it meant to be a neighbor. Coincidentally, through his work with Inter-Varsity, Percy was studying racial reconciliation. He and Angie wondered what it might be like to be a neighbor in a neighborhood where they were among the minority.

The next thing they knew, they were packing up their comfortable apartment and moving into a run-down Greek Revival townhome in the heart of Richmond's Church Hill neighborhood. Like many other U.S. urban neighborhoods, Church Hill declined in the 1970s and '80s. The black middle class and the majority of whites moved away, leaving only a very poor black population. With no money, limited skills, and little education, many of the neighborhood's residents turned to cocaine, heroin, and crime. John Johnson, a past president of the neighborhood association, once described Church Hill in the early '80s as the "drug-infested shooting gallery of Richmond." In her book on Richmond's historic neighborhoods, preservationist Mary Wingfield Scott remarked that, by the early 2000s, Church Hill had "sunk to near slum condition."

When Percy and Angie moved to Church Hill in the summer of 2000, the neighborhood was struggling more than ever. "What have we gotten ourselves into?" they thought. Gunfire and drug deals were routine. One evening, Percy heard a string of shots followed by loud screaming. He ran to his front door and saw a man crawling up his porch steps. As the gunfire continued, Percy ducked out the door and pulled the stranger onto his porch, yelling frantically, "Call 911!" The shooter jumped into his car and sped away. Suddenly, the man on the porch stood up, thanked Percy, and walked away. He had feigned being shot to fool the shooter into thinking he was dead.

Dodging crime and trying their best to acclimate to a new world, Percy and Angie didn't do a whole lot of neighboring when they first arrived in Church Hill. They did, however, manage to make a few inroads with the kids in the neighborhood. It started when Percy first visited Bill Robinson Park, a neighborhood hangout with an outdoor basketball court. In his silly style, Percy would arrive at the court with his basketball, his farm-boy whiteness, and his not-so-serious game face. He made sure to learn the names of everyone he met, from the youngest child to the oldest adult. After a few afternoons of doing this, Percy found that people were starting to warm up to him. "Here comes P-Dawg!" they said. Even though Percy always played basketball hard, he kept his games fun and light at the park. The people of Church Hill couldn't help but start to like him. Percy saw them as human beings and neighbors—first and foremost— rather than criminals.

A surprising ritual began after each basketball game: when Percy started walking home, the neighborhood kids would follow him. He remembers the first time they followed him—even though he had said goodbye more than once—laughing and giggling all the way to his front porch. Percy and Angie offered the kids some food and video games, and soon they were coming over at all times of the day. Percy and Angie would sometimes come home to a group of fifteen kids sitting on their front porch.

One day, Percy—who was trying to imagine a way to reframe the situation—said to the kids, "Hey, guys, maybe eating all my food and playing video games isn't the best option you have here." The kids looked at each other and laughed. Then, to Percy's astonishment, they shared with him what they had recently been thinking about: tutoring. The kids asked whether it would be possible for Percy and Angie to help them with their homework.

Later that night, the couple talked about the kids' request. They had moved to Church Hill to learn how to be good neighbors; maybe this was their chance. After thinking and praying about the idea for several nights, Percy and Angie began opening their home two afternoons a week for tutoring sessions. Each week, ten to fifteen kids would come by for help with their homework. Connections started to form, and the kids began to feel a real excitement about learning. They relished the attention they received, and word spread quickly around Church Hill about the sessions.

As the tutoring continued into the winter of 2001, Percy knew that he needed to make sure that fun was a part of the group's experience. So on Valentine's Day, 2002, he threw a roller-skating party at a local rink for the kids and their families. The kids had a blast, but the parents had their walls up. Here was this white guy who had barged into their neighborhood and was now shaking up their kids' lives. Percy kept chipping away, though, one wall at a time, with the same sociable attitude. At one point, a mother confessed to Percy that she had initially thought he was an undercover police officer working for the City of Richmond. She had thought that he was running a major sting operation on Church Hill, and that Angie was an actress playing his wife. Percy and the mother laughed hysterically about it.

Percy didn't get to know everyone at the roller rink that day, but it was a step in the right direction. In Percy's mind, if he could exist in the community, not as an outsider, but as a neighbor, then more adults would become more open and something incredible might happen.

The tutoring and fun rolled on through the summer of 2002. Percy's and Angie's friends started volunteering to help. The group was quickly growing in size, and there were some growing pains. One day, Percy and his friends took the kids to Kings Dominion, an amusement park just thirty minutes from Richmond. Knowing that none of the kids had ever been there, and that most were incredibly poor, Percy funded the whole trip on a home-equity line of credit. When they got there, the kids were afraid of the rides and wanted to leave after only a couple of hours.

Another time, Percy was short on tutors, so he said, "Let's just go to the park and play kickball." After explaining the rules to the forty kids who had never played kickball before, Percy separated them into two teams. Things looked promising, until one girl kicked a questionable foul ball down the first-base line. The opposing player at first base rudely yelled, "Foul!" Before Percy could react, the girl who had kicked the ball was charging the other team. Pandemonium broke out, and both teams began wrestling each other. Luckily, the brawl ended as quickly as it had begun and everyone was okay.

Despite these and other small tests along the way,

momentum for Percy's and Angie's tutoring was positive. Through various activities like summer barbecues, Percy continued to build relationships with the community of Church Hill. Ultimately, in 2002, the nonprofit organization Church Hill Activities and Tutoring (CHAT) was born.

Percy never thought that Andy's challenging question would result in the founding of a nonprofit organization, nor could he come close to comprehending everything that CHAT would become over the next decade. Today, CHAT consists of nearly forty-five paid staff members, hundreds of volunteers, multiple homes providing tutoring services, a preschool, a high school, and a nearly $2 million operating budget. Over the past thirteen years, CHAT has been nothing short of transformational for the kids in the Church Hill neighborhood. Every Valentine's Day, CHAT celebrates its birthday with a fun activity and a big party. Every summer, the group goes to Kings Dominion, because now the kids love it. During the summer of 2014, more than 200 kids attended, and many of them stayed until the park closed. As for the infamous kickball fight, it has become a playful part of CHAT's history, fondly dubbed "CHAT's Kickball Riot."

When asked what he thinks is different in Church Hill compared to when he first moved to the neighborhood over a decade ago, Percy says that everywhere you go, you know someone. He also notes more friendly banter and a sense that everyone is watching out for everyone else. It seems like "there is a different soul to the neighborhood," he says. Alexandra Franck, a woman who recently moved to the neighborhood, describes it similarly:

"I have literally never experienced anything like this. Everyone here is involved a little bit in each other's lives." A hip culinary scene has also started to evolve, bringing outsiders to the neighborhood. Church Hill has even received national attention, with *USA Today* naming it one of the top ten most up-and-coming neighborhoods in the country in May 2014—a giant leap for a community that was near slum condition.

Percy would never want to take credit for the renaissance that has occurred in the Church Hill neighborhood since CHAT started, but it's hard to see how anything else has been more instrumental. Other things have certainly helped, including an aggressive historic preservation effort, tempting tax breaks for new businesses, and a revitalization of religious organizations in and around Church Hill.

But perhaps the best indicator of what has happened is to look at the crime statistics. The table below represents crime data for the Church Hill neighborhood from 2000 to 2014, gathered from the City of Richmond's police department database (page 69).

Crimes directly involving others include homicides, sexual offenses, robberies, and burglaries. Crimes indirectly involving others include vice crimes, thefts, and other miscellaneous crimes. It's not hard to notice the trend toward less crime in both categories. But when you look closer, you'll see that the trend begins in the early 2000s—right when CHAT was gaining traction.

Percy and Angie now have four birth children and two older children from Church Hill whom they adopted several years after moving to the neighborhood. Looking

YEAR	CRIMES DIRECTLY INVOLVING OTHERS	CRIMES INDIRECTLY INVOLVING OTHERS
2000	124	469
2001	160	446
2002	123	452
2003	157	468
2004	115	371
2005	91	328
2006	114	371
2007	87	309
2008	66	286
2009	63	275
2010	50	251
2011	64	239
2012	47	283
2013	46	202
2014	55	192

around, nobody in Church Hill is thinking, "Hey, there is Percy, the CEO and founder of CHAT." They are thinking, "Hey, it's Percy. I have to stop in and talk to him. I have to hear the latest story of how he embarrassed himself or his latest parenting failure." This is exactly how Percy likes it. Because that kind of sociability is what helps people, including himself, feel a sense of community and connectedness.

When asked what he sees for CHAT in the next ten years, Percy hopes the Church Hill youth of today take over the reins of the organization. "We knew we were doing things right when the youth started saying things like, 'Well, when I run CHAT, this is how things are going to be,'" Percy says. "I hope that's what happens. If it does, my work will be done here."

●━━━●

On the surface, it may seem that playful sociability is just about being friendly and easygoing with other people. But it's probably more accurate to describe it as a tendency to connect with others in a mutually beneficial way. Or, as Percy's story shows us, it means being the best "neighbor" we can be. The big questions are: How exactly do playfully intelligent people accomplish this, and what can we learn from them that will help us make good on our own social investments?

I found two consistent themes throughout my research and interviews that speak to these questions: 1) playfully intelligent people seldom apply preconceived notions about the people with whom they are engaging and, likewise, seldom form strong first impressions during their social interactions; and 2) playfully intelligent people usually approach their social interactions with humility and powerlessness, and this manifests as a strong sense of egalitarianism.

While Percy was integrating into the Church Hill neighborhood, he exemplified both of these themes at a high level. He saw the residents of Church Hill as people rather than criminals. He also knew that sometimes a criminal is a criminal not because he or she desires to hurt others or society, but because he or she has nowhere else to turn. Growing up on his family's farm and learning from his grandfather's example of sociability, Percy also understood the importance of seeing others as equal and either pushing beyond initial impressions and judgments or resisting them altogether. Likewise, Percy never takes himself too seriously, which is, in many ways, his gateway to living a humble life.

Let's look at these two themes a little deeper, starting from a place that is very familiar to me: the bedside.

An effective physician must be able to determine, with infallible accuracy, the disease (or diseases) ailing his or her patients. While compassion and empathy are essential for good doctoring, most patients (and physicians) would say that making a correct diagnosis is the most important task of the physician. In this sense, physicians-in-training spend a significant amount of time learning the science of diagnosing diseases.

Introduced early in medical training, and practiced fiercely as that training progresses, the foundation of this science is a process called *differential diagnosis*. In this process, the physician generates a list of possible diagnoses, from most to least likely, that could explain the patient's clinical state. Similar to brainstorming, the more diagnoses on the list, the better—at least, initially. Beginning with the patient's story, the physician uses clues to build the list. Then, homing in on the two or three most likely diagnoses, further evaluation—through a physical exam or laboratory, radiological, and/or procedural testing—helps the physician arrive at the working diagnosis on which treatment is based.

The intent of differential diagnosis is to move the

physician toward the correct diagnosis and also prevent
him or her from falling into the psychological trap known
as *anchoring bias*. First introduced in 1974 by psychologists Amos Tversky and Daniel Kahneman, anchoring
occurs when we place too much value on the initial pieces of information or data presented to us. When we do
this, the information itself becomes a stubborn starting
point—an anchor—for our thinking. As more information
is gathered, we either confirm that our anchor is correct,
or try to adjust our thinking away from it.

But, as Tversky and Kahneman discovered, herein lies a problem: it's hard for us to adjust our thinking
once our brains start anchoring. They first described this
problem in the context of making judgments under uncertainty, such as performing numerical estimations. For
example, they asked study subjects the percentage of
African countries in the United Nations. Before answering, participants were randomly assigned a number from
0 to 100. Tversky and Kahneman then asked whether
the subjects thought the percentage was higher or lower
than their number. The random number (which became
a subconscious anchor in the participants' minds) had a
marked effect on the participants' answers: the median
estimates of the percentage of African countries in the
United Nations were 25 and 45 for groups that received
the random numbers of 10 and 65, respectively.

In another demonstration of anchoring bias, Kahneman
and his colleague, David Schkade, asked Midwesterners
and Californians to rate their own happiness as well as
which group they believed was happier overall. They found
no statistical difference in self-rated happiness between

the two groups, but both groups believed Californians were happier. When they looked at the data, Kahneman and Schkade found that people placed significant value on California's favorable climate, equating it to greater happiness. Translation: the study subjects weren't able to adjust away from their climate anchors.

In medicine, anchoring happens when a physician immediately thinks he or she knows the correct diagnosis. The physician holds onto an initial symptom and then quickly anchors on one disease *without* using differential diagnosis. A good example of this that I have seen involved a patient who suffered from long-standing heartburn caused by stomach acid refluxing into her esophagus.

"My reflux is acting up," the patient told her physician. "I'm having a lot of heartburn and chest discomfort, and TUMS aren't working." She asked if there was anything else she could take besides Prilosec (an acid-reducing medication). Failing to dig beyond the initial, seemingly obvious diagnosis of worsening gastroesophageal reflux disease, the physician prescribed another acid-reducing medication and sent the patient on her way.

Later that night, the patient felt worse and went to the emergency room. Her evaluation revealed a life-threatening pulmonary embolism, another disease that can also cause significant chest discomfort. Fortunately, she survived. Had her physician not anchored on the diagnosis of worsening reflux and instead worked through the process of differential diagnosis, he would have been more likely to ask the patient about recent trips, a risk factor for blood-clot formation in the legs and subsequent pulmonary emboli. The patient had just returned from a business trip to China.

Anchoring bias has been studied in many different contexts since Tversky and Kahneman's initial description, from economics to decision-making to medicine. In Daniel Kahneman's book *Thinking, Fast and Slow*, he describes two different systems that our brains use to think, and places anchoring within this construct. The first system, which Kahneman calls System 1, is responsible for fast, intuitive, automatic, emotional thinking. This system allows us to escape danger by forming quick first impressions. System 1 is responsible for our gut instincts—but also for anchoring.

The second system, System 2, controls slow, deliberate, logical thinking. It is the skeptic and critic inside us, helping us work through difficult problems. Not surprisingly, System 2 requires a significant amount of mental energy and effort, while System 1 uses less mental energy. Most of the time, System 1 gets it right—human intuition is quite accurate. But, as Tversky and Kahneman discovered, problems arise when System 1 doesn't get it right; it's very hard to move our thinking away from misplaced anchors.

The way in which System 1—and the anchoring that's associated with it—relates to the playful quality of sociability boils down to stereotypes and first impressions. In our social interactions, especially with people whom we have just met, System 1 is rapidly trying to make sense of the person in front of us. One way it does this is through what sociologists call *categorical person perception*, or *stereotyping*. System 1 invokes the mental shortcut of stereotyping to speed up the process of getting to know someone. Why? Efficiency is everything for the brain. By running with the initial information it receives, the brain saves energy. And without conscious effort to the contrary, the brain will use as many mental shortcuts as possible. The brain is an incredibly lazy and inattentive organ in this sense.

Sometimes the stereotype is cultural, and sometimes it stems from someone we have met in the past or someone we know who is similar in appearance or character to the person in front of us. No matter where they come from, stereotypes, whether positive or negative, are a big part of any society or culture. But when we leave false stereotypes unchecked in our brain and they get repeated over and over again, they become hardwired into our System 1 thinking and end up clouding our perception.

Is stereotyping uncontrollable? As you might imagine, a half-century of worldwide positive momentum for civil rights has prompted considerable debate surrounding this question. Up until about fifteen years ago, stereotyping had been viewed as automatic and unavoidable. The amount and extent to which our brain used stereotypes depended on how much cumulative exposure (hardwiring) we had for the stereotypes at hand.

Recently, however, extensive evidence has suggested that with conscious mental effort—via System 2—we can successfully inhibit stereotypical processing in the brain, no matter how hardwired it is. Interestingly, though, "conscious mental effort" doesn't mean that we necessarily need to think, "This is a stereotype I shouldn't use." Rather, it means that when we are occupied (cognitively busy) with another aspect of what is in front of us and occurring in the moment, stereotyping is less likely. For example, if we are having a conversation with a person and our brain begins to stereotype that person, we might focus on the goal or purpose of the conversation to avoid stereotyping. If we remain in the moment and give the other person our full attention, listening closely to what he or she is saying, our brain's natural instinct to stereotype will subside.

Ultimately, when we meet someone we don't know, or even someone we do know, System 1 is trying to decide whether that person is friend or foe. It's doing a lot to figure this out, from reading body language and vocal tone to using stereotypes. If System 1 is successful, it will quickly establish its first-impression anchor. But the longer System 1 takes to form a first impression, the more likely it is to fail. And when System 1 takes a long time or fails, a first impression may still form, but it will do so with the helpful influence of System 2.

People like Percy, with high levels of playful intelligence, rarely form first impressions during their social interactions. And if they do, they don't place a high intrinsic value on them. They also approach each of their secondary and tertiary (and so on) impressions with a blank slate, carrying forward very few appraisals from their past interactions. Simply put, System 1 stereotyping and judging, in any context, is significantly reduced during a playfully intelligent social interaction. This helps those involved avoid the assumptions that often divide us.

sociability—humility—playfully intelligent people take themselves less seriously on average and, in turn, usually communicate in nonthreatening, humble ways. Humility, according to Merriam-Webster, is the quality or state of not thinking that one is better than someone else. Percy certainly didn't think he was better than his Church Hill neighbors.

In his book *Give and Take*, Adam Grant, a management and psychology professor at the University of Pennsylvania Wharton School, describes what he calls *powerless communication*. He notes that powerless communication has four central tenets: 1) vulnerability; 2) listening; 3) tentative talk; and 4) advice-seeking. Paradoxically, these four tenets combine to give powerless communicators great power.

As Grant explains, those who use powerless communication can build rapport, trust, and influence much more efficiently than those who adopt a *powerful* style of communication (e.g. strong opinions, closed statements, and ultimatums). Of the four tenets, vulnerability, expressed through humility, is the one that is most apparent in the social interactions of playfully intelligent people.

One additional example worth highlighting surfaced serendipitously during my investigation of the Illinois Bell story presented in Chapter 1. While I was learning about how imaginative, transformational coping helped some of the Illinois Bell employees thrive during AT&T's divestiture, I stumbled upon the story of John Zeglis.

Like Percy, John grew up in a small, farming town— Momence, Illinois, located just south of Chicago. John's family didn't have a farm, but they surely lived a simple,

humble life. As one of three boys, John enjoyed playing sports, especially basketball and golf. He was also
a great student, graduating as valedictorian of his high
school class. His father, Donald, was the town's lawyer.
Donald instilled in John the values of hard work while
having fun along the way, and always meeting people
where they are.

John studied business at the University of Illinois
and eventually made his way to law school at Harvard.
In 1973, he came back to the Midwest, accepting his first
job as an attorney at Sidley Austin in Chicago, where he
was tasked with helping to manage Sidley Austin's AT&T
account. Given the political climate surrounding AT&T,
John knew that the assignment would be challenging. He
also knew that the telecommunications industry was foreign soil for him. But by the late 1970s, John had become one of Sidley Austin's lead attorneys, helping AT&T
navigate its antitrust lawsuit and impending divestiture.
Fortunately for him, and for AT&T, John did a great job.
In fact, today he is largely credited with safely routing
AT&T to the other side of divestiture.

As John moved AT&T past a very difficult time in
its history, his good-natured personality, humility, can-
dor, and intelligence caught the eyes of AT&T's brass.
After the breakup of the telecommunications giant, John
was tapped to serve as AT&T's general counsel. This position afforded John a seat at AT&T's executive table.
John would later recount, "I learned a lot about business
strategy, sociability, and leadership while I sat at the big
table—or an open chair in the corner of the room!—answering the many legal questions that naturally surfaced

for our FCC-regulated company."

In the late 1990s, AT&T's board of directors faced the problem of the succession of longtime CEO Robert E. Allen. Its initial hire of Allen's handpicked outsider, John Walter, CEO of the printing company R. R. Donnelley & Sons, was a disaster. Within a matter of months, the board told Walter that he wouldn't ascend to the top chair when Allen stepped down. Walter resigned upon hearing the news, and the board was back to square one.

The Walter misstep and years of turmoil in AT&T's executive ranks alienated many senior executives, leaving the board with very few internal options to replace Allen. After completing another round of vetting, the board narrowed its list to one external candidate, Michael Armstrong, CEO of Hughes Electronics, and one internal candidate, John Zeglis. John humbly recalls, "I was basically the last 'in-house' person standing."

By this time, John was known for his brains (he had become one of the company's chief strategists) and playful sociability. One of his trademarks was carrying around Trivial Pursuit cards wherever he went. He had gotten the idea from his father, who also carried the cards around. John remembers cleaning out his dad's car after he died, only to find two things in the trunk: piles of unused AT&T prepaid long-distance calling cards and boxes of Trivial Pursuit cards. John made a habit of leaving the cards in AT&T's corporate jets. The object of the game was to always work as a group, never against one another, to see how many questions out of seven cards could be answered correctly. With six questions per card, each question was worth one point. A perfect game, answering all forty-two

questions correctly, was worth forty-two points. Teams
would scribble their scores on the sides of the game boxes
for bragging rights.

John knew that the biggest hurdle standing between
him and becoming CEO of AT&T was his lack of operational experience. Although he had gained some in the
interim after Walter stepped down, he had virtually no experience in running a company. But in true John fashion,
he kept his humble wits about him. "I never hid the fact
that I had no CEO experience or was embarrassed about
it," he says. "Sure, I wanted the job, but I also wasn't
about to pretend I was someone other than who I was."
The board eventually hatched a hybrid solution, making
Armstrong CEO of AT&T and John president of AT&T, as
well as CEO of the spinoff service AT&T Wireless. Although he could have easily played the role of sore loser,
John graciously embraced his new position, continuing to
show his humble sociability.

John retired from AT&T in 2004, but not before he
had made many lasting contributions to the telecommunications industry. Perhaps the most influential was ignit-
ing the rise in popularity of text messaging in the United
States. This was catalyzed by AT&T Wireless's early part-
nership with the reality television show *American Idol*.
As millions of Americans used text messaging to vote for
their favorite singer each week, AT&T saw a dramatic
increase in overall text-messaging rates. What was happening? By using text messages to cast their *American
Idol* votes, people became more comfortable with texting,
and more likely to text their family and friends. The rest
is history.

Not surprisingly, John never hogs the credit. He always shares it. "I was surrounded by a lot of smart people, and we had fun working together." Considering John's humility, this approach fits. In fact, it's very common among successful executives. Leadership guru Jim Collins, who has interviewed thousands of thriving executives, explains it like this:

> Throughout our interviews with high-performing executives, we were struck by the way they talked about themselves—or rather, didn't talk about themselves. They'd go on and on about the company and the contributions of other executives, but they would instinctively deflect discussion about their own role. When pressed to talk about themselves, they'd say things like, "I hope I'm not sounding like a big shot," or, "I don't think I can take much credit for what happened. We were blessed with marvelous people."

To this day, when John is asked what it was about him that he thinks worked for AT&T, he responds with humility. "By sheer dumb luck, I was right in the eye of the storm of every major controversy in telecommunications in the last quarter of the twentieth century," he says. "I consider myself the Forrest Gump of the telecommunications industry! I was really swept along. After a while, the company ran out of presidents."

I would take it a step further and say that if this is true, then John played a role in creating his own luck. And assuredly, his seasoned sense of playful sociability is far from trivial.

●——●

To quickly recap, the playfully intelligent use two guiding themes during their social interactions. First, they approach their social experiences with an "anchors aweigh" mentality, limiting knee-jerk, stereotypical impressions of others. Second, they are humble during their social interactions, which is a direct extension of their overarching lighter take on themselves and the world.

The second half of this chapter is going to take these lessons and attempt to answer the questions: "So what? Does this translate to anything beyond healthy social relationships?"

But before we get there, it's worth clarifying one issue. If you're an introvert, you might be saying to yourself, "This isn't me. I don't really like to socialize with other people." Or if you're an extrovert, you could be saying, "I got this." The truth is, we are all introverts *and* extroverts to varying degrees. Believing that we are solely one or the other is self-limiting. I'm not trying to say to the introverts, "Get out more," or to the extroverts, "Keep on keeping on." I'm saying that we are all social beings. Even the most extreme introverts need to exist, to some extent, in close, warm, loving connection with other people—not isolated and alone. And even the most extreme extroverts need to step back every now and then and examine how they are being sociable.

So do the themes of playful sociability—anchors aweigh and humility—translate to any specific benefits? The obvious answer is that they are likable characteristics.

Nobody wants to be judged, or spend time around someone who is narcissistic and arrogant. We tend to like those who aren't judgmental and who exude modesty. But is something deeper going on? Let's take a closer look.

Seymour Sarason, a Russian Jew, grew up in the early 1900s, in the Brownsville section of Brooklyn. Looking down from his family's apartment window, young Seymour saw a bustling, urban community made up of just about every race, nationality, and religion. From men pushing two-wheeled ovens, claiming to have the best chestnuts and sweet potatoes, to women peddling carts of colorful fruits and vegetables, Brownsville's harmony fascinated Seymour.

When he was six years old, his family moved to Newark to be closer to extended family. In Newark, surrounded by his Jewish family and their friends, Seymour's Jewish identity began to take shape, complementing his urban one. Now, when he looked at the streets, he saw kosher meat markets, Jewish bakeries, and Jewish fish and candy stores.

In 1942, after graduate studies in psychology, Seymour went to work at a state mental institution called Southbury, located in rural Connecticut. Most of Southbury's residents were impoverished minorities who had an intellectual disability (IQ equal to or below seventy). The Southbury model, similar to that of most other mental institutions across the country at the time, was to remove people from their families and communities, bring them to the country for training and education, and then return them home.

Early on, Sarason recognized that the residents didn't

feel as though they belonged at Southbury. He noted how
they often felt lonely and adrift. If they weren't trying to
escape, they were fixated on their memories of where they
came from. Sarason also noticed how the staff at Southbury usually viewed the residents through a diagnostic
label (i.e., IQ below seventy) and referred to them as
"children," no matter how old they were. They were anchored in the perspective that the residents were unintel-
ligent and nonfunctional.

Sarason suspected that he, too, could be anchoring,
so he administered a test to the Southbury residents with
the hope of finding some answers. In the test, the residents looked at a series of pictures and created a story. The test was designed to show an external reflection
(the story) of the resident's internal world. What Sarason
found was that the residents thought about and yearned
for loved ones, and they reacted to forced separation with
bewilderment, dejection, and despair.

After seeing the test results, Sarason started approaching the residents differently. He began to view his
relationship with them as he viewed his relationships
with his friends, colleagues, and family. He also remembered the communities that he had been a part of, what it
was like to be "a stranger in a strange land," and how important a sense of community was to his and his family's
well-being. He began meeting and interacting with the
residents more openly, asking them about their families
and the communities they had come from. Southbury's
staff followed Sarason's lead and an improved experience
for Southbury's residents was forged.

Sarason would ultimately move on from Southbury to

pioneer the field of community psychology. Rather than focusing exclusively on a person's internal psychiatric problems, Sarason looked at factors affecting one's community, including poverty and depression, and how one's sense of community affected his or her life. He initially described one's sense of community as "the feeling that one is part of a readily available, supportive, and dependable structure, that is part of everyday life and not just when disasters strike." With Sarason's inspiration, many psychologists and sociologists followed suit in the years to come, investigating what it takes for one to feel a sense of community.

The most widely accepted model for understanding this was put forth by David McMillan and David Chavis in 1986. The model describes four components that contribute to a sense of community: *membership, influence, integration and fulfillment of needs,* and *shared emotional connection. Membership* means having boundaries to determine who is an appropriate member of the community and who is not. Members must feel that they matter, or have a certain degree of *influence* within the group; then they must feel relevant, rather than replaceable. *Integration and fulfillment of needs* means that the community must reinforce the individual in some way. *Shared emotional connection* is the glue that holds the community together.

A good example of this model in practice is a well-functioning older-adult living community. More often than not, the people living in these residences know who the other members are, and they feel a sense of influence from their involvement in community activities. These living communities also reinforce their individual members, and those members share an emotional connection.

According to McMillan and Chavis, when these four elements intersect, a sense of community develops. Although all four elements are probably needed for one to experience a sense of community, the one element that McMillan and Chavis call "the definitive element for true sense of community" is shared emotional connection—the glue. And to create the glue, McMillan and Chavis say there must be *contact* and *high-quality interaction* between the parties involved.

Contact means that the more people amicably interact, the more likely they are to become close. *High-quality interaction*, which is more critical than quantity of contact, relates to the importance of the experience to those who share it. McMillan and Chavis underscore one critical part of a high-quality interaction: emotional risk. They say that "the amount of interpersonal emotional risk one takes with the other members and the extent to which one opens oneself to emotional pain from the community life will affect one's general sense of community."

As it turns out, the sociable actions of playfully intelligent people align with what McMillan and Chavis say is necessary for a high-quality interaction. When one puts aside his or her judgments and arrives at a social interaction in a powerless, vulnerable, humble way, he or she has a better chance of having a positive, high-quality interaction, which means a better chance of experiencing shared emotional connection and, in turn, a sense of community. Take, for example, twelve-step programs such as Alcoholics Anonymous. Participants are encouraged to come to meetings completely powerless, vulnerable, and humble. As stories of struggle are shared against the backdrop of these principles, participants not only experience shared emotional connection and a sense of community, but also make positive steps toward recovery.

What's more, playfully intelligent people use their imagination to step into another person's shoes, as described in Chapter 1. This capacity for empathy also increases their odds of social success. McMillan and Chavis call it *shared history*, and believe that it is another important part of shared emotional connection. They say that "it is not necessary for group members to have participated in the history in order to share it, but they must identify with it." Identifying with someone else's history calls on one's imagination to find similarities, to better understand and empathize with that other person. A good example of this is when parents share parenting stories with other parents. Even though the parents listening to these stories may not have experienced the exact same situations with their own children, they can identify with the stories (and the parents sharing them) by placing their child into the paradigm that's building in their minds.

So as we resist anchoring, remain humble, and imagine what it would be like to be the other person, a shared emotional connection with others takes hold, and our sense of community improves. This answers the "So what?" question. The ways that playfully intelligent people are sociable—anchors aweigh and humility—greatly foster their sense of community.

This sense of community is important for obvious reasons and some not-so-obvious reasons. It helps us combat

feelings of social isolation and loneliness, both of which
are risk factors for premature death, with negative impacts on adult health that are comparable to high blood
pressure, lack of exercise, obesity, and smoking. But
there's more.

Traditionally, the benefits of sense of community have
been organized and studied according to the types of communities that people commonly belong to. On a practical
level, classifying these communities into simple categories helps one become more aware of how exactly each
community is affecting his or her overall sense of community. The three community categories that I like to use
are *family*, *neighborhood*, and *beyond*. While there is certainly overlap, these categories correlate geographically
to within our home, just outside our home, and everything
else beyond our neighborhoods; the *beyond* category is a
grab bag of different communities (e.g., workplace, social, spiritual, etc.).

On a *family* level, one's sense of community is most
strengthened when his or her family is spending time together, caring for one another, and being playfully sociable in a nonjudgmental and humble way. Unfortunately,
the bustling life of today's American family doesn't leave
much time for consistent togetherness. One exception to
this rule, however, can be family meals.

Many American families make eating together a priority because it's hard to connect in other ways during
the week. A family will usually share dinner together,
and maybe breakfast, but rarely lunch. Gallup has been
tracking family-meal frequency since 1997. On average,
just over half of U.S. families eat dinner together six to

seven nights out of the week. Another third do so four to five nights per week. Interestingly, adult-only families eat together at about the same rate as adult-child families.

This is all good news because the sense of community that comes from making family meals a habit goes a long way toward improving physical, mental, and emotional well-being. Among a host of other benefits, family meals lead to higher self-esteem, a greater sense of resiliency, a lower risk of depression, and lower rates of obesity. Youth who have regular family meals are more motivated at school, perform better academically, and get along better with their peers.

So if you feel as though your family is living a crazy-busy lifestyle, think about whether family meals are happening with predictable frequency. They are a good place to start exercising your sense of community, and they make a big difference for everyone in the home.

Next, stepping away from the dinner table to just outside the front door, one's sense of community can also be impacted by his or her *neighborhood*. It's certainly true that our neighbors might not be our friends (some may even seem like our enemies!). But the truth is that just an inkling of neighborhood cohesion can positively influence one's mental and physical health.

One of the most studied examples of this is the small Italian-immigrant town of Roseto, Pennsylvania. In the 1950s and 1960s, Stewart Wolf, a physician-scientist at the University of Oklahoma, spent his summers near Roseto. One day, a local physician relayed a curious observation to him: the people of Roseto who were under sixty-five didn't seem to have heart disease. Wolf investigated this peculiarity and found that, indeed, the death rate from heart disease was half of that found elsewhere in the country, at least for men under sixty-five. Rosetans also seemed to be living longer than one would expect.

This didn't make sense to Wolf. The average Rosetan ate poorly, was obese, and smoked. Why were the people of Roseto less prone to heart disease? With the help of sociologist John Bruhn, Wolf began to see what could be working in Roseto's favor. He noticed how close-knit the community was. People regularly took time to talk to each other and have meals together. There was a feeling of belonging in Roseto. You knew that you could come to your neighbors for help. There were also at least twenty community organizations in Roseto that promoted social interaction and bonding.

After looking at all the data, including genetics, Wolf and his colleagues concluded that it was Roseto itself, and the social support and sense of community that the town's residents offered one another, that made the difference. Interestingly, Wolf and his team later found that the effect disappeared as Roseto became less tightly knit in the 1960s. They examined death certificates for Roseto and the nearby town of Bangor, Pennsylvania, from 1935 to 1985. Although Rosetans had a lower mortality rate from heart attacks over the course of the first thirty years, it rose to the level of Bangor's after experiencing a period of decline in family and community cohesion.

Since the Roseto study, many others have looked at the relationship between neighborhood cohesion and health. The majority of these studies have found that

social connections between neighbors, including greater social cohesion and neighbors helping other neighbors, are protective against depression. They have also
revealed that less social cohesion in a neighborhood is
associated with worse self-reported health. As far as heart
disease and mortality go, it appears that neighborhood
togetherness does decrease one's risk of cardiovascular
disease, but it's unclear whether death rates are affected.
Similarly, it's unclear whether health behaviors, such as
smoking, drinking alcohol, and eating poorly, are affected
by one's neighborhood.

Does this mean that we should be throwing more
neighborhood block parties and bringing homemade
cookies with us to share every time we take a walk down
the street? No, of course not. But small actions in the
neighborhood could go a long way toward building a
sense of community—such as knocking on your neighbors' doors to introduce yourself, like Percy did. Or taking more moments for small talk in the neighborhood, and
not dismissing those moments as a waste of time. Whatever form that sense of community takes, we will be better
off once we start to build it.

Finally, the category of *beyond* encompasses all the
other communities that we belong to. These communities include our circle of friends, our workplace and the
coworkers we interact with, and our spiritual communities. They also include our social, athletic, and support
groups, civic and volunteer organizations, and, last but
not least, our virtual communities. Like our family unit
and our neighbors, these other groups also help nurture
our sense of community, especially when we approach

other members of the community with the playful sociability themes of anchors aweigh and humility in the fore-
front of our minds.

In today's age of technology, virtual communities are
more relevant than ever. Do virtual communities afford us
true connections and provide comparable benefits to the
sense of community that comes from our brick-and-mor-
tar, face-to-face communities? To answer this question,
it helps to first understand, on a physiological level, why
in-person social connection is beneficial. When we are
in close physical proximity to someone with whom we've
formed a connection, or when we receive genuine physical affection from someone else, our brains release the
neurohormone oxytocin.

Produced in the brain's pituitary gland, oxytocin was
initially studied because of its role in lactation and uter-
ine contraction. But it has since been discovered that
oxytocin is also critical for social bonding. When it is released—via a simple fist-bump, handshake, pat on the
back, or even a gentle nudge—it tells us that the other
person is present and ready to listen, or cry, or laugh with
us. Because of this important role that it plays, along with
its role in sexual arousal and monogamy, oxytocin has
been crowned the "cuddle" and "trust" hormone. In some
ways, the release of oxytocin supports the *contact* part of
the equation for shared emotional connection.

In the virtual world, we presumably lose the oxytocin effect (although more research is necessary to confirm
this). What then becomes most important is whether our
virtual connection is of *high quality* (the other half of the
equation for establishing a shared emotional connection).

If we are habitually heading to Facebook or Twitter to escape our current reality or perhaps receive affirmation from it, then the answer is probably "no." But if we are simply checking in or sharing with the people we know and have connections with in the real world, then the virtual connection could feasibly be experienced as a high-quality interaction, benefiting our sense of community. In other words, the effects that our virtual communities have on us, and the extent to which they help grow our sense of community, depend largely on our intention and awareness.

Unfortunately, the addictive nature of social media makes sustained awareness challenging. When we receive a "like" or comparable positive feedback through our social media communities, the nucleus accumbens (the brain's reward center) is activated and dopamine is released. This makes us feel good and crave more quick, positive feedback. The nucleus accumbens also plays a role in processing the gains in one's social reputation. The more people who acknowledge us in our virtual communities, the more we think that our reputation is improving.

But this leads to what is known as the *Internet paradox*. The paradox questions whether time spent online keeps us from making connections with real people or conversely allows people who are shy or socially uncomfortable to connect with others. Although the answer varies from person to person, research on Facebook users suggests that Facebook use correlates with a general decline in well-being over time for young adults, potentially contributing to feelings of loneliness. Compounding the problem is that if one feels lonely or lacks social support, he or she is more likely to look to Facebook for encouragement. Putting these two data points together, if you are feeling lonely, the tendency may be to look for connection online, which could backfire in the long run.

Two interesting twists to this story involve at-risk teens and older adults. It appears that exposing at-risk teens to various community-based websites via social media helps the teens learn how to use the Internet in a positive way. One example of this was shown for young men at risk for HIV. By learning about HIV testing and resources through various virtual friends and community pages on Facebook, young men at risk for HIV were more likely to request HIV testing kits.

For older adults, Facebook use may diminish cognitive decline by nearly twenty-five percent. Recognizing this potential benefit, companies such as Ages 2.0 and Connected Living have incorporated technology training into nursing homes, allowing residents to connect with various online communities such as Facebook. This type of programming seems to heighten feelings of self-competence, personal identity, and cognitive capacity—all leading to better mental health and well-being.

So it seems that with our virtual communities, what's most important is the awareness we bring to our screens and devices. If we are already feeling lonely and turn to the virtual world, we run the risk of worsening our situation. That may be the time to connect with someone face-to-face or on the phone. But if we approach our virtual communities with the right intentions, and an openness to form shared emotional connection, our sense of community is likely to be strengthened. Sharing a moment online with a childhood friend living across the country is most likely going to be beneficial, and if that connection occurs with abandoned judgment and humility, we stand poised for a high-quality interaction and a nourishing of our sense of community. As we have learned, a healthy sense of community can be largely driven by playful sociability that limits anchoring and maximizes humility. When, little by little, we become more attuned to how we are being sociable and to the communities that are patiently awaiting our attention (family, neighborhood, and beyond), we are able to deepen the shared emotional connections we already have, piece together new, meaningful ones, and enjoy the benefits of the company of others.

I'll let one playful patient have the last word here, since the proof is often in the pudding.

Gloria M.'s ninety-seven-year-old heart had failed once again, landing her in the hospital for a few days. The extremely narrow opening in her aortic valve had caused fluid to back up into her lungs and even her legs. The medical team had begun giving her medication to help remove the excess fluid and give her heart a boost. This would be the hospitalization during which she would need to consider having her heart valve replaced.

One morning, as the medical team prepared for bedside rounds, one of the medical students noted, "She is a very functional ninety-seven. She looks like she's sixty-seven. She goes bowling with 'The Ladies.'" The team entered the room to find Gloria propped up in bed, lost in an apparently delightful thought. Her shoulder-length, stringy gray hair and oversized Coke-bottle glasses made her look cartoonish. Instead of the standard thin cotton hospital gown, Gloria wore a thick pink wool cardigan over a blue-and-pink flowered nightgown.

"Good morning, Mrs. M.," said the attending physician. "How are you feeling?"

"I'm feeling good," Gloria replied. "Can't complain."

"Now, Mrs. M., I think we have some wrong information on our charts. It says you are ninety-seven. I think we may have added twenty years or so to your age!"

Gloria shrugged her shoulders and cocked her head to one side. Having heard it so many times before, she replied through a sheepish smile, "No. I'm *ninety*-seven. I still go bowling! Twice a week!"

"Are you any good?" asked the attending.

"I'm good enough. My average is a seventy-one." (Gloria played candlepin bowling, for which a seventy-one is pretty darn good!)

"So, what's your secret?"

"Oh, I don't know," Gloria responded.

She acted as though she had been asked this question hundreds of times, but she wasn't giving up her wisdom that easily. Realizing that quantity of life doesn't supersede quality, Gloria's vibrant spirit spoke to a remarkable, sustained quality of life that she was still enjoying in spite of her weary heart valve.

"Do you not worry?" the attending inquired.

"No, I worry a lot."

"How about your diet? Do you eat only vegetables?"

"No, I eat everything."

"Not that many sweets?"

"No, I eat sweets."

"Do you smoke? Drink?"

"I don't smoke or drink. At least I haven't for years."

"Hmmm . . . it must be the bowling, then," the attending concluded.

Gloria's face lit up as she looked directly into the attending's eyes, winked, and replied, "You bet!"

Sociability Well Played

Anchors Aweigh

In social situations, anchoring happens when one falls back on stereotypes, forms erratic impressions, and jumps too quickly to conclusions and judgments about the other person. This usually equates, at a minimum, to a missed opportunity for shared emotional connection and the benefits that such a connection affords.

Appropriately named, anchors are heavy and hard to reposition. The key is to avoid anchoring in the first place. Here are some pearls that can help:

- **Shift focus.** A common trigger of social anchoring is one's mental focus on the notable differences that may (or may not) exist between him or her and the other person. It's easy to zoom in on perceived differences in attractiveness, financial worth, and prestige. When we do this, anchoring is more likely to occur and harm the social interaction. The next time you catch yourself focusing on differences, try shifting your focus toward something you like about the other person or something you have in common.

- **Embrace a mood swing.** The happier we are, the less we tend to anchor. This makes sense because when we are more content, we are less likely to judge both others and ourselves. Sometimes it's difficult to completely

change our moods, but just thinking of something that
makes you happy, even for a few seconds, can decrease
your anchoring risk. Consider taking a quick moment
to indulge in a comforting or happy memory before your
next social interaction. This will help keep your anchors stowed away.

• **Accept the anchor.** Given how hard it is to avoid anchoring altogether, it's fortunate that not all anchoring
is bad. Impressions can be spot-on. Simply becoming
more aware of when you are anchoring can help you
recognize whether it may be limiting your relationships. With practice, you will be able to quickly identify whether the anchor you dropped is preventing your
relationship from setting sail.

Powerless Communication

A critical part of playful sociability and playful intelligence is being vulnerable, humble, and open during social exchanges. This happens, in general, when we take
ourselves less seriously, and specifically when we make
powerless communication a defining aspect of our social
styles. Here are some tips that will help make powerless
communication, and humility, a habit:

• **Listen more (especially to women).** In his book
Give and Take, Adam Grant describes how Jim Quig-
ley, former CEO of Deloitte Touche Tohmatsu, decided
to work on his powerless communication by setting a
goal to talk no more than twenty percent of the time

during his meetings. This helped him shift his answers to questions as well as gain a better understanding of people's needs. Try setting a similar goal for yourself during your next social interaction. Also, women naturally tend to use powerless communication styles more often than men. So whether you are a man or a woman, if you are looking to improve your powerless communication skills, look (and listen!) to women to find best practices.

- **Reframe opinions into suggestions.** One very effective way to use powerless communication is by taking an opinion and using your imagination to reframe it into a suggestion, possibly in the form of a question. For example, rather than saying, "I think the best way to solve this problem is to spend more money," you might say, "I wonder whether more financial resources could help solve this problem." Reframing opinions into suggestions keeps the conversation a two-way street, and allows people space to gently push back if they don't agree with you.

- **Competence first.** Adopting a more powerless style of communication may result in becoming more passive, which can have some benefits, particularly if your natural style tends to be more aggressive. Being passive, however, can sometimes allow one's performance to lapse. This can land you on the wrong end of what is known as the *pratfall effect*: that those who recognize their mistakes or blunders will be more or less highly regarded depending on their perceived competence. Those who are perceived as generally competent will be more liked for their awareness of their shortcomings, while those who are perceived as less competent will be less liked. In other words, powerless communication works best when your humble approach is paired with your capabilities, strengths, and competence. You remain powerful, but in a more controlled, humble way. John Zeglis referred to this as "intellectual gravitas first," which, in his line of work, meant that he first needed to demonstrate his competence in the eyes of AT&T's stakeholders *before* his humility and playfulness could be seen in a positive light.

CHAPTER THREE

Humor

In 1959, finding someone who was reading *The Magic of Thinking Big* was as easy as finding a jukebox in a local diner. Written by David Schwartz—a psychology professor at Georgia State University—*Thinking Big* was a wildly popular self-help book, which contended that the principal force holding people back in their lives was the smallness of their thoughts. Thinking small meant not believing in oneself or simply shooting for less than the stars. Schwartz argued that if we could understand how our thought processes worked, then we could use them to think big and achieve proportionate goals. While he was right on several levels, his ideas were also flawed. Mainly, he didn't foresee how his message would be interpreted in the context of the late 1950s.

It was fifteen years after World War II, the United States was the world's superpower, and consumerism was fashionable. Americans equated big thinking and big success with materialism: owning a home, a car, a boat— bigger and better than what the Joneses had. Americans were also getting really good at playing "happy," even when they weren't actually feeling that way. Bottling up stress was a way of life, and the perfect scenario depicted in the classic 1950s television sitcom *Leave It to Beaver* became the fairy tale of millions across the country.

The reality lurking beneath the surface was very different. For average Americans, life was becoming increasingly complex, serious, busy, stressful, and competitive. With their coping skills stretched, Americans watched their individual identities—not to mention their ability to know themselves and relate to one another—slip away. Top-heavy and tumbling, the mindset of thinking big needed a course correction—fast.

The big and bigger themes of the day were a boon for the advertising industry. New York City's Madison Avenue, the advertising capital of the world, was an exciting and prosperous place to work. But one small ad agency, Doyle Dane Bernbach (DDB), was doing everything it could to stay afloat. With a lousy national ranking of eightieth, it was the equivalent of a hot dog stand on Madison Avenue (maybe two hot dog stands).

Ned Doyle, Mac Dane, and Bill Bernbach—three young guys—had opened the agency's doors on June 1, 1949. At thirty-eight years old, Bernbach was the youngest of the three, but he was the brains behind every move. One close associate once said of Bernbach: "He's wideeyed and curious. He has a great sensitivity to what people will feel in first impressions, and he has complete faith in himself." Bernbach enforced only one rule: tell the truth. If you thought an ad created by one of your partners missed its mark, then you had better speak up.

Bernbach also believed that the client *wasn't* always right. He wanted his team to trust their work and rely on their intuition. Most important, he thought ads should be designed for their intended audience, not the client or product. Bernbach watched people reading newspapers and magazines on their subway ride home, noticing that most weren't giving advertisements even a quick glance. The secret, which Bernbach realized before the rest of the advertising world did, was that at the end of a stressful day, the last thing you wanted to see were beautiful, smiling people in front of products that you didn't have, or perfect lives that you knew didn't exist.

Even though Bernbach's finger rested on the pulse of materialism's empty promise, and he understood that Americans were trying to live up to unattainable, storybook lives, the agency still struggled. In 1957, an unconventional DDB ad for El Al Israel Airlines helped moved DDB out of hot-dog-stand status. But—perhaps caught up a little in the mysticism of the "more" lifestyle himself—Bernbach still felt that DDB was missing one thing: the Big Account.

In the early 1930s, Adolf Hitler had dreamed of providing German citizens with an affordable car—a "People's Car," which translated to *Volkswagen* in German. Ferdinand Porsche, who by that time had become widely regarded as a genius in automotive design and engineering, shared his dream. In 1934, Hitler asked Porsche to design his People's Car, and Porsche developed what would become the Volkswagen Beetle.

Before many Beetles could be made, however, World War II broke out, and the Volkswagen plant in Wolfsburg,

Germany, halted Beetle production. When the plant was bombed by British troops toward the end of the war, the Beetle seemed destined to go down with the rest of the country—and it would have, if not for the leadership of Heinrich Nordhoff. The British assigned Nordhoff—a German industrial lawyer and experienced production man—to salvage any materials that remained and to determine whether Porsche's little car was worth further pursuit. As a smart industrialist, Nordhoff quickly realized that Porsche had been on to something, and in three short years he resurrected the plant and gave the Beetle a fresh start.

Across the Atlantic, the American market for the Beetle was beginning to pick up, but at a slower pace than in Europe. Detroit's automotive Big Three took notice and launched three compact cars of their own: General Motors had the Corvair; Ford, the Falcon; and Plymouth, the Valiant. To counter Detroit's move, Volkswagen and Nordhoff decided that for the Beetle to survive in the United States, they had to do something drastic, something they'd never really done before—advertise.

Carl Hahn, a brilliant economist and chief of Volkswagen's export sales, was charged with finding a U.S. advertising agency. He knew that he needed an exceptional one because Americans were not yet friendly to foreign cars—especially the Beetle, which most people identified with Hitler, the Nazis, and the war. Its unusual, compact design also diverged from the contemporary American auto taste of "bigger is better." Still, word spread quickly on Madison Avenue that a European automobile company was shopping for representation.

At first, Hahn was disappointed in what Madison Avenue had to offer. As he would later note, "We had looked at about a dozen agencies, and they all made huge presentations to us in extravagant boardrooms. But all we saw were Volkswagen ads exactly like every other ad—an airline ad, a cigarette ad, a toothpaste ad. The only difference was that, where the tube of toothpaste had been, they'd placed a Volkswagen."

But when Hahn finally showed up in DDB's office, all those earlier disappointments seemed to work in DDB's favor. "Bernbach didn't make any presentation in the proper sense. He just showed us work that DDB had done for other clients and explained to us his way of thinking," Hahn recounted.

Bernbach and Hahn hit it off, and Hahn chose DDB. But despite a good connection between the two men, Volkswagen allocated only $800,000 for Beetle advertising in the United States—a far cry from what was needed for the Beetle to compete on foreign soil. DDB needed to pull off an advertising miracle.

Bernbach knew who he wanted on the Beetle campaign: George Lois and Helmut Krone would create the art, and Julian Koenig would write the copy. From the start, there was a lighthearted rapport among the three colleagues. Keeping the mood humorous was their way of handling the fact that they were working on a German account. When Lois and Koenig visited the Beetle plant in Germany to learn more about the car, they marveled and joked about such things as the millionth Beetle, a gold bug with shimmering rhinestones, and Volkswagen's strange-looking military jeeps. At an evening dinner party, using one of their dinner napkins as home plate, they entertained their hosts by demonstrating the American baseball slide in the middle of the dining hall.

In response to America's obsession with big, more, and happy, other agencies were producing automobile ads that featured luxurious photographs, beautiful people, and opulent backgrounds. The three jovial colleagues had a different approach in mind. In the spring of 1959, Koenig came to Krone's office to share the text he had drafted for the Beetle ad. It was written in a childlike tone and had a touch of humor, with comments such as "the Beetle had become as American as apple strudel." Krone and Lois took Koenig's copy to the drawing board and returned with a tiny picture of the Beetle in the upper left side of the page, surrounded by only white space. On the bottom of the page in small type was Koenig's copy below the headline: "Think small."

Bernbach's Beetle team had gone against every rule of advertising. Their approach was tongue-in-cheek instead of serious, used white space instead of picturesque imagery, and featured small text rather than enormous lettering. It was humorous, too, and humor in advertising was more taboo than accepted. The late Claude Hopkins, who was perhaps the greatest copywriter in the history of the industry, once boldly pronounced, "People do not buy from clowns!"

The Think Small ad ran in *Life* magazine in February 1960. It was an instant success. As the playful anti-ad, it cut through the plastic showiness of the period's typical advertisements. Because of Think Small, the Beetle would become one of the first icons of 1960s counterculture—a bubbly, colorful reminder to never take life too seriously. To this day, Think Small is considered the best ad campaign ever, ranked by *Advertising Age* as number one in the century's top 100 campaigns. Why did Think Small work? In part, it suggested a new way of thinking about not only advertising, but life itself. You didn't have to be the best, biggest, or seemingly happiest: genuine contentment could be found in the simple and small. The other, equally important aspect of Think Small was that it spoke to the playful child inside everyone. Its lighthearted approach reminded Americans—amid the intensity of the day—that a little playfulness and humor could make a big difference in their lives.

●——●

By now, after working (and playing) your way through Imagination and Sociability, you may notice your perspective on playfulness beginning to change. If this is the case, I hope the momentum continues. But if you haven't noticed a shift yet—stay ready. With its outward expression of laughter, humor is perhaps the most recognizable playful quality that we have. Of the five that are explored in this book, humor is by far the most synonymous with playfulness. In fact, one might even say that having a sense of humor is equivalent to having a sense of playfulness. I like to think of humor as simply another part of the playful intelligence equation, in which all five playful qualities contribute in different ways to living lightly.

Over the last forty years, many people have taken humor to the anatomy lab. The end result is always the same: as American essayist E. B. White put it, "Humor can be dissected, as a frog can, but the thing dies in the process, and the innards are discouraging to any but the pure scientific mind." Suffice it to say, my goal for this chapter is to keep the playful quality of humor breathing for you until the end. I also hope that you come away with a slightly different take on the subject—one that will make humor a more tangible and valuable resource for you. I like to believe that this is kind of what happened to Americans living in the 1950s, when Think Small subtly changed their thinking.

By now, you could probably guess that I think playfulness should be regarded just as earnestly as, say, healthy eating and exercise. This is really the great paradox of this book: adult playfulness is actually *serious* business, and it needs to be valued and respected as such.

Taking humor seriously may seem like a contradiction of terms; after all, humor helps us bring levity to our experience of the world, and of each other. This is certainly true on the surface. But when you think about how much humor could actually be affecting your life and well-being, it becomes clear that it is much more than just a seriousness minimizer.

To fully understand this, it's helpful to first look at the relationship between humor and health. Once we do this, it will quickly become clear how playfully intelligent people most often use humor in their lives.

Up until the late 1970s, the scientific community paid little attention to the relationship, if any, between humor and health. Everything changed in 1976 when Norman Cousins, an American political journalist and magazine editor, published an article in the *New England Journal of Medicine* titled "Anatomy of an Illness (as Perceived by the Patient)." The article, which Cousins would later expand into a best-selling novel, described Cousins's diagnosis of ankylosing spondylitis, a condition that causes severe inflammation and pain in the vertebrae. Rather than seeking the standard treatments available at the time, Cousins checked himself into a hotel and spent several days reading joke books and watching *Candid Camera* and Marx Brothers movies.

As the story goes, Cousins made a full recovery from ankylosing spondylitis, and he gave the lion's share of the credit to those days he spent laughing at the hotel. Cousins's recovery spawned a plethora of research on humor's impact on health and well-being. Nearly four decades later, hundreds of studies and experiments have been conducted to clarify the relationship between humor and health.

From a physical health perspective, the domains studied most have been humor's impact on the immune and cardiovascular systems, as well as its moderating effect on physical pain. Of these three, humor's pain-reduction effect has the strongest supporting evidence. It's likely that laughter chemically triggers a reduction in the perception and experience of pain.

The immune system is the body's defense against all things programmed to destroy it, such as infections and cancers. So it would be great if humor benefited the immune system, but the data isn't conclusive. Some experiments have found that, as study subjects watched humorous videos, they experienced an increased expression of immune-system molecules. It's difficult to know, however, whether these increases have any real health benefits, in the short or long term. There is certainly no downside to thinking that funny videos may benefit the immune system, as long as viewing them doesn't replace proven therapies. It's like the old Jewish joke that goes:

> A Rabbi delivers the eulogy at a man's funeral.
> Old lady in the back row: "Give him some chick-
>   en soup! Give him some chicken soup!"
> Rabbi: "Madame, it wouldn't help."
> Old lady: "It couldn't hurt!"

Similarly, research suggests that humor benefits the cardiovascular system. It appears that laughter may be associated with short-term elevations in heart rate and blood pressure, analogous to what happens during exercise. But it's unclear whether these transient effects afford any concrete health benefits. By the same token, a sense of humor may portend a protective effect against coronary heart disease, the major cause of heart attacks. But the data is murky at best. Nevertheless, since heart disease is the number-one cause of death in the world, it's tough to argue against a little harmless laughter, as long as it is combined with more tested therapies and interventions.

Perhaps the ultimate way to evaluate whether humor affects physical health is to examine its relationship to longevity—the summary metric of physical health. The best study to date on this relationship was published in 2010 by Sven Svebak and his colleagues at the Norwegian University of Science and Technology. Over seven years, more than 60,000 Norwegians participated in the study, which attempted to control for factors that influence or may influence life span, such as education, exercise, smoking, social network, body-mass index, systolic blood pressure, kidney function, diabetes, cancer, and cardiovascular disease. The results supported the notion that a sense of humor may increase the likelihood of one living to the age of sixty-five. But beyond sixty-five, there was no obvious effect on survival. The research team hypothesized that, after age sixty-five, other factors, such as genetics and biological decline, likely have a greater effect on longevity. The big confounder in the study was that most of the data came from self-report and survey techniques, which can be prone to error.

All in all, the evidence that humor can give us a physical health advantage is at most only suggestive. The research is far from definitive, and in many cases, the methodologies used in the studies lack the scientific rigor that is needed to draw noteworthy and solid conclusions.

But there's more to overall health than just the physical condition, of course. It's true that the field of medicine has traditionally concerned itself mainly with physical health, and that society also tends to focus on physical health—that is, one's *quantity* of life or longevity. But the mental aspect of health and, in turn, one's *quality* of life is just as important. No one wants a long life that's full of despair.

This brings us to the cusp of how playfully intelligent people tap into and use the power of humor in their daily lives.

In early May 2007, Howard Davies-Carr, an information technology consultant living with his family just west

of London, England, decided to shoot some home video of
his sons, three-year-old Harry and one-year-old Charlie.
The brothers sat together on the family's leather reclin-
er, with Charlie in Harry's lap, facing the camera. Without warning, Charlie, who had about seven teeth poking
through his gums, began to nibble on Harry's index finger. Harry, caught by surprise, giggled and announced,
"Charlie bit me!" as he pulled his finger back to safety.
Eager to experiment, Harry then purposefully put his index finger back into Charlie's mouth, and Charlie instinc-
tively clenched down on it.

At first, Harry laughed. But as Charlie's bite intensi-
fied, Harry's face turned to one of mild panic as he began
screaming, "Ouch, Charlie! Ouch! Charlie, that really
hurts!" Harry managed to get his finger out of Charlie's
mouth. Startled by Harry's screaming, Charlie appeared
as though he was about to cry. But then he broke out into
a huge jack-o-lantern grin and let out a big laugh. Harry
inspected his finger for damage, and then, in the climac-
tic moment of the video, also smiled and laughed to signal
that he was okay.

The entire exchange lasts fifty-five seconds. On
May 22, 2007, Howard uploaded the video onto YouTube
so that his father, who was living in Colorado at the time,
could see his grandsons in action. The video, now affec-
tionately known as "Charlie Bit My Finger—Again!,"
went on to become one of the first viral videos ever. Since
its debut, it has accumulated over 800 million YouTube
views and in 2017 ranked eleventh on the list of most-
viewed YouTube videos of all time.

What exactly was it about this video that made it go

viral? Jonah Berger, a marketing professor at the Wharton School at the University of Pennsylvania, has researched this question as part of his work on how social influence causes products and ideas to catch on. Berger found that content which induces a high-arousal state is more likely to be shared from one person to the next.

In one interesting experiment, Berger randomly assigned participants to view either a low- or high-arousal version of an advertising campaign for Jimmy Dean sausages. In the low-arousal version, Jimmy Dean hires a farmer to be the spokesperson for the company's line of pork products. In the high-arousal version, Dean hires a rabbi as the spokesperson (this is designed to provoke humor because pork is not considered kosher). Berger then asked each group how likely they were to share the campaign with others. Sure enough, the group that viewed the high-arousal version was more likely to share it.

Berger's research tells us that we are more likely to share content with others if it stirs emotion. In the case of "Charlie Bit My Finger—Again!," the viewer is taken through several arousing emotions all at once, with humor being the net effect.

But how does this relate to how the playfully intelligent use humor in their lives?

Funny videos have the potential to go viral because we want others to feel the emotions that we are feeling, even if only for a brief moment. When this happens, our *connections become stronger*. Humor, whether it's in the form of a shared video or a shared laugh, can be a channel for building connections; it says to others that it's safe to explore, play, and nurture a relationship together. And herein lies the first of two important ways that playfully intelligent people use humor in their lives. Howard not only wanted to provide a glimpse of Harry and Charlie to his dad—he also wanted to *connect* with his dad.

In my clinical work, I haven't seen my patients experience any direct physical health benefits from humor, but I have seen how humor can open the door to connection for them.

●━━━●

Vivienne described her upbringing in Manila, the capital of the Philippines, as "pretty regular." She was the fourth of six children, and her childhood play was standard fare: dolls, climbing trees, pretend cooking, and adventures on the playground. When she was seven, however, her mother died unexpectedly from a heart attack, leaving her father and his *yayas* (the Filipino term for a nanny) to rear the children.

Vivienne's father was a stern Chinese Buddhist. She remembered seeing and hearing him laugh only after he had a few beers under his belt and was telling an outrageous story. These times were rare, though, and seriousness was his default. Vivienne thought that maybe her father was this way because his wife had died so young. Maybe he had never found a consistent rhythm. Nonetheless, Vivienne felt loved and cared for.

In her early twenties, Vivienne worked as a cashier at Nino Deroma's, the only Italian restaurant in Manila. One afternoon, a handful of young, hungry American men popped in. With an unusually large smile, one of the men approached Vivienne and asked, "How fast can you have a pizza made?"

The man's name was Dan. Dan worked as a commercial diver in Brunei, but was vacationing in Manila with some American friends. Mesmerized by the petite, beautiful Filipino woman behind the cash register, Dan wasn't just salivating over the smell of fresh pizza. As he described it, "There was and still is something about Vivienne." Unable to keep his eyes off her, he smiled every time she looked up from the register's keys. His pleasantries that afternoon, however, were to no avail; Vivienne didn't reciprocate. Taking the hint, an unrequited Dan headed back to Brunei.

Six weeks later, Dan was in Manila again and took a taxi straight to Nino Deroma's. This time, he was determined to ask Vivienne out. He sat down at a corner table that offered the perfect view of his Filipino crush. Vivienne wondered if there was something wrong with this vaguely familiar American man who kept grinning boyishly at her. She approached Dan, who had just ordered a soda, and asked, "Do I know you?" Spellbound, Dan mentioned that he had been in the restaurant a few weeks earlier. Then he started throwing out some jokes. Luckily for him, by now Vivienne was learning to laugh a little easier and more frequently. Dan's humor caught her attention.

Dan asked Vivienne to have dinner with him that night, to which Vivienne jokingly responded, "We're not supposed to date our patrons!" But then she whispered in his ear, "Meet me on the corner at seven o'clock."

His head buzzing with romance, Dan floated back to his hotel. At dusk, he took a taxi to the restaurant and waited on the corner, smiling nervously from ear to ear. As Vivienne came around the back of the restaurant and made her way toward Dan, his smile shrank. Two men— neither of whom was smiling—flanked Vivienne. They were Vivienne's brothers! Fortunately, the dinner went perfectly—for all four of them. Family chaperones would be the norm for Vivienne and Dan's first year and a half of dating, but Dan took this in stride. He was more than willing to do whatever was necessary for the chance of winning Vivienne's affection forever.

Dan relocated to Manila, and the two rented an apartment next to Vivienne's aunts and cousins. Being the only American in Vivienne's small community, and knowing that Vivienne's family surrounded her with protection and love, Dan maintained a high level of good behavior. But he also stayed true to himself. His cheerful manner, sense of humor, and perpetual smile helped the locals overlook his idiosyncrasies, including his subpar grasp of the language.

One afternoon, Vivienne sent Dan out for some milk. Dan asked one of the market workers where he could get his hands on some fresh *susu*, the Malaysian word for milk (Malaysian is spoken in Brunei). The worker giggled and pointed to the cooler. When Dan got home, he told Vivienne about his request. She started laughing uncontrollably, informing Dan that the word closest to *susu* in Tagalog (the language spoken in metro Manila) is *suso*, which means "breast."

Vivienne and Dan wed in the Philippines and eventually made their way to the United States, settling in Massachusetts. The couple and their relationship continued to grow when they arrived in America, and humor continued to be a big part of their love story. Unlike Vivienne's childhood, playful banter had been commonplace in Dan's formative years. He remembered the innocent jabs exchanged between himself and his parents and the situational jokes that he and his friends kept alive for months. It wasn't until Dan was older, however, that he really started to appreciate humor's deeper value. As cracking harmless jokes became a habit, Dan started to see how humor could help him connect with others. He saw how it helped people, including himself, drop their personal walls and engage more openly and vulnerably during conversations. Dan's favorite person to connect with was, of course, Vivienne. His jokes kept her laughing, which kept Dan joking. Singing loudly out of tune, blackening their teeth with makeup, and giving their friends silly nicknames were some of Vivienne and Dan's favorite tricks.

But it wasn't always fun and games. Vivienne and Dan knew when life called for the kind of seriousness and intensity that Vivienne had experienced growing up—such as in 2008, when she noticed that she was becoming more and more short of breath. Her medical evaluation revealed rheumatic heart disease from untreated strep throat during her childhood. Her aortic valve was leaking, and blood was backing up into her lungs. The valve needed to be replaced.

Vivienne had open-heart surgery on her aortic valve. It went well, and Vivienne was home five days later. But five *years* later, she began having trouble breathing again. Now it was her mitral valve. She had a second open-heart surgery, and this time things didn't go well. During the operation, her heart went into shock. Her blood pressure plummeted, and she was rushed out of the operating room to the intensive care unit (ICU). Multiple medications, called pressors, kept her blood pressure normal and Vivienne alive. Typically, patients who need pressors receive them for one or two days while the cause of low blood pressure is identified and treated. Vivienne was on pressors for twenty-four of the thirty-two days she spent in the ICU. Her hands and feet became black and gangrenous because her blood vessels were constricted everywhere in her body, leaving the tissues in her hands and feet starving for oxygen.

Amazingly, Vivienne survived the ICU and was transitioned out of the hospital into a rehabilitation facility. When you ask Dan about Vivienne's time in the ICU, he will tell you in a shaky voice, "Viv tried dying on me several times. *Several.*" When she arrived at the rehab center, Vivienne had a tracheostomy tube coming out the front of her neck, a catheter in her chest for dialysis, and a feeding tube in her abdomen. Her tubes, drains, and lines weren't atypical for a patient transitioning to rehab from a hospitalization that included intensive care. The rehab team knew this. What they didn't know was the impression Vivienne would make on them.

Right from the start, Vivienne's inner warmth and laughter spread to those around her, giving everyone energy. Not being able to speak clearly because of her tracheostomy tube, Vivienne always smiled and laughed at herself as she fumbled through her scribbles of questions in her notebook (she could barely hold a pen with her gangrenous fingers). She also told the rehab staff about how much she enjoyed the little things, like smelling an orange. This helped the staff remember to appreciate the little things in their own lives. She told her nurses about the dangers of looking too far ahead, and talked to them about how important it was to focus on small, attainable goals, such as being able to eat yellow Jell-O again—the goal that Vivienne set for herself on the day she arrived. "Must it be yellow, Ms. Vivienne?" the staff asked her. "Only yellow!" she screeched back. Everyone was always laughing with Vivienne.

After nearly three months of intensive daily therapy, Vivienne's tracheostomy and feeding tubes were removed. She started eating again, beginning with her prized yellow Jell-O. By that time, she had also become a regular Mario Andretti on her burgundy electric scooter—"The Viv Mobile," as she called it. She maneuvered through the hallways and rooms with a speed and precision that had never been seen before on the rehab circuit. As she cruised the halls, the staff pretended that they were hitchhikers, only to get the classic Vivienne look that said, "Eat your heart out—you can only dream of riding on one of these!"

Naturally, some setbacks accompanied Vivienne's rehab milestones. Because of her gangrene, she required below-the-knee amputations of both of her feet, as well as her left hand and most of the fingers on her right hand. True to form, Vivienne didn't use the standard assistive devices that most people in her situation use. Rather, she created some of her own adaptations, like a gigantic pair of tweezers. "Viv's Claws" allowed her to move things around.

Vivienne laughed hard as she recalled her prosthetic

legs coming loose in the pool during aqua therapy. "Help! My other half is floating away!" she hollered to her therapists. Dan smiled when he recalled the afternoon of laughter that he and Vivienne shared with the staff after he had taken a photo of Vivienne's prosthetic legs dangling over the edge of the shower. "My legs, my legs! I must remember my legs!" read the caption. Through humor, Vivienne and Dan built strong connections with the rehab staff, and they knew that they could count on each other.

Vivienne would relearn how to drive, cook, and paint, despite being told that her chance of ever being able to do these things again was small. Her remarkable recovery spoke to all the wonders of physical rehabilitation that she experienced, but it also spoke to the power of humor.

At the beginning of their relationship, humor was a way for Dan to bridge the cultural divide between himself and Vivienne. For Vivienne, Dan's humor was a breath of fresh air in the midst of her upbringing. While she attributes her humor awakening to Dan, Vivienne has also brought lightness to Dan's life by laughing easily at his jokes and showing, by example, how it's best to not take oneself too seriously. As the years have gone by, the two have made sure that humor is a priority in their relationship and in their relationships with others, too. They say it best when asked about some of the ways that they experience humor together:

> We always watch movies that are inspirational or funny. We also watch the Hallmark Channel, just because it's nice. We also try to pay attention to the kind of people and friends that we surround ourselves with. We like to be around people who

have a sense of humor. Life is too short to do it
any other way.

If you ask Vivienne and Dan about using humor to
connect with others, they will tell you, "We're not necessarily always making jokes when we are with people. We
know when to be serious. It's more about looking at things
lightly and humorously. Perhaps having a low threshold
for laughter, too. It's how we have always lived."

As her rehabilitation came to a close, Vivienne's love
(and obsession!) for "therapeutic ironing" prompted the
staff to hang a sign that read "24-Hour Laundry" above
the facility's laundry-room door. Now, every time they
see the sign, the staff also sees Vivienne—ironing away,
eating yellow Jell-O, cruising on her scooter, using her
claws, and, of course, laughing.

•———•

Humor scientist Rod Martin defines *affiliative humor* as
"an interpersonal form of humor that puts others at ease,
amuses, and improves relationships." This is the type of
humor that Vivienne and Dan frequently use, and it often
brings down the walls that can exist between people, providing space for connections to develop.

I call this kind of humor "healthy humor." Unlike sar-
casm, aggressive teasing, self-defeating humor, or other
unhealthy forms of humor, healthy humor produces positive results—like better connections with others. And it
follows one guiding principle: that humor shouldn't make
other people feel bad. Instead, it should make us feel

good, happy, and connected.

When I first started looking at people's senses of humor, I thought that playfully intelligent people would be really funny—always telling jokes and, more often than not, making light of life. Surprisingly, I didn't find this to necessarily be true. Rather, as in the case of Vivienne and Dan, I found playfully intelligent people to be masters of healthy humor. Although not necessarily funnier per se, they seemed to commit fewer humor mistakes during their interactions. In other words, playfully intelligent people seemed to be experts at steering clear of unhealthy humor, with the vast majority of their humorous exchanges being rooted in healthy-humor constructs.

An analogy in the game of basketball is when someone says that a basketball team "doesn't make mistakes." This means that the team rarely commits turnovers, such as throwing the ball out of bounds or dribbling improperly. From an athleticism standpoint, this team may not be the most skilled or athletic team on the court, but it commits fewer errors. Similar analogies can be found in other sports, such as tennis, with its unforced-error statistic. The idea is that, even though one may not be very funny, just a little humor that's served in a healthy way can enhance one's connections.

But how exactly do playfully intelligent people minimize humor mistakes during their social interactions? How do they keep the basketball and the tennis ball in bounds?

I've found that the answer to this question boils down to safeguards; playfully intelligent people use (sometimes consciously and sometimes subconsciously) various safeguards to reduce their risk of engaging in unhealthy humor. For example, recall how the playful quality of imagination can be used to put oneself in the shoes of others. When it comes to humor, this imaginative empathy helps playfully intelligent people see where another's offensive line is. By seeing this line quickly and clearly, playfully intelligent people are less likely to cross it when they are being funny.

Similarly, recall the humble aspect of playfully intelligent sociability that was discussed in Chapter 2. It is this humility—the kind that Percy Strickland and John Zeglis showed—that often manifests as self-deprecating humor. Self-deprecation is nonthreatening and vulnerable. It allows other people in, and it's also unlikely to be offensive.

In other words, by being able to imaginatively see the out-of-bounds line, and using self-deprecating, humble humor, the playfully intelligent safeguard themselves against unhealthy humor exchanges.

I've also found that playfully intelligent people laugh a little easier on average, which is another safeguard for them. This doesn't mean that they laugh inappropriately or excessively. It just means that, given a set of potentially humorous circumstances, they are more likely to laugh than not. Their laughter keeps the mood light and playful, which promotes healthy humor. As someone who laughs very easily, Vivienne is a great example of this.

Interestingly, a low laughter threshold is linked to the biology of how we connect with each other. Humans most likely started talking to one another in order to establish and strengthen social bonds. Since a conversation can include only so many people, laughter is thought to have developed as a way of engaging and bonding with a larger group.

The area that controls laughter in the brain is the subcortex, which also contains structures that are responsible for automatic behaviors like breathing and muscular reflexes. The subcortex is considered the nonthinking part of the brain. Laughing easily (or, in a sense, automatically) can be considered humans' built-in survival mechanism to signal that it's safe to connect and bond with each other.

Dr. Robert Provine, a neuroscientist and professor of psychology, has researched this concept extensively over the course of his career. Observing people in natural settings like parks, sidewalks, and malls, Provine found laughter to be more about relationships than humor. He noted that we are thirty times more likely to laugh in social situations than when we are alone. He also found that most adult laughter does not follow jokes, but instead punctuates speech, often occurring at pauses.

Another safeguard against humor blunders that I observed in playfully intelligent people is the notion of deliberately exposing oneself to humor. It may seem trite, but in the majority of my interviews and observations, I found that playfully intelligent people put a high value on experiencing humor in their lives. Whether it's humor supplied through media, performance, or relationships, the playfully intelligent make time for and value funny experiences. This helps them continually polish their understanding of what healthy and unhealthy humor is.

It's an interesting question to ask oneself: "Do I value

humor enough to consciously and deliberately spend time with it?" When I have asked this question of others (and myself), I found that most people value humor in terms of its intrinsic worth, but this value doesn't necessarily translate into how we prioritize humor during our leisure time. Actions always speak louder than words—one can say that he or she values humor, but rarely seek it out at the same time.

When people are asked in formal research studies whether they value humor, most respond in the affirmative (who wouldn't say that he or she values humor in his or her life?). For example, both men and women rank humor as one of the top traits they seek in a mate. By the same token, ninety-one percent of executives deem a sense of humor in the workplace to be important for career advancement; eighty-four percent believe people with a good sense of humor do a better job; and eighty percent think humor plays an important role in being able to successfully integrate into corporate culture.

So we say that we value humor, but are we actually deciding to spend time with it? Are we becoming students of it, in a sense, to better understand how it works and better position it for good in our lives? These questions haven't been directly studied, but there is some indirect data that can offer at least partial answers.

According to the U.S. Bureau of Labor and Statistics, Americans spend an average of 5.26 hours a day doing leisure-related activities. This number has stayed constant, in the five-hour range, over the past ten years. Although we don't know how much of that leisure time is spent on humor-related activities, television-watching is the top leisure activity, accounting for roughly half (2.8 hours) of our leisure time each day. Socializing is second, accounting for about fourteen percent (43 minutes) of our leisure time each day.

Looking at socialization first, as we saw in Vivienne and Dan's story, we should be considering someone's sense of humor or lack thereof when a friendship or romantic relationship is brewing. It's important not only for relationship longevity, but also when thinking about how much time we are actually spending with humor.

As for television-watching, the question is whether we are spending time watching funny shows. The best data on this comes from Nielsen, which showed that sitcoms ranked last in overall primetime viewership from 2001 through 2011. Reality shows and drama were the two most popular genres. An interesting twist on this data is that the order is reversed when it comes to viewership on airplanes. People are more likely to watch a streaming comedy on the in-flight entertainment system than reality or drama programming. Do we seek humor more often when we are detached or relaxed, such as on a trip or vacation, as opposed to when we are still plugged in? It's difficult to know for sure, but regardless, our goal should be to value humor enough that we consciously choose to spend time with it, even when we aren't at 30,000 feet.

What about comedy clubs and funny movies? Data on comedy club attendance is scant, but one recent study conducted in the United Kingdom found that half of the surveyed population attended a comedy club at least once a year. In terms of movies, of the top 100 grossing movies of all time, only the *Shrek* series cracks the list as a comedy. Similarly, in the Academy Awards' eighty-seven years, only six comedy films have won the coveted Best Picture award: *It Happened One Night* (1934), *You Can't Take It With You* (1938), *Going My Way* (1944), *Tom Jones* (1963), *The Sting* (1973), and *Annie Hall* (1977). Ultimately, when it comes to spending time with humor, it really doesn't matter what the data suggests. What does matter is whether you personally feel that you are deliberately spending time with humor, and whether you are able to identify what healthy humor looks like when it's front and center. If the answers are "Not enough time" and "Not sure," then that might be a cue to seek out a little humor more often.

Having grown up in the 1980s, my all-time favorite comedy movie is *Ferris Bueller's Day Off*. If you've never seen it before or haven't watched it recently, it's worth a look. When I need some inspiration to prioritize humor more in my life, I often draw on Ferris's most famous line from the movie: "Life moves pretty fast. If you don't stop and look around once in a while, you could miss it." The line reminds me to seek out humor in my daily life.

The playfully intelligent use their imaginations to see the offensive lines, pepper their sociability with self-deprecation, laugh easily, and seek out humor—all to give their own humor the best chance at helping them connect with others.

As we will see in the second half of this chapter, the connecting force of humor segues nicely into the other equally important force that humor imparts on the lives of the playfully intelligent: resiliency.

Perhaps Ferris should have also said that when

life moves frighteningly fast—too fast for us to even
breathe—a laugh or two can sometimes give us a little air.

●——●

For Brenda Elsagher's thirty-ninth birthday, she and her
friends celebrated at a comedy club in the Mall of America in Minneapolis, Minnesota. Brenda loved comedy, and
she herself had a great sense of humor that put people at
ease. It came from her father, Eugene, who was the clown
in the family. Eugene, or "Hump" (after Humpty Dump-
ty) for those who were close to him, used many puns and
also told funny stories, the kind that brought people to
tears. One of his classic jokes was to whisper to dinner
guests, "You know, you're really hogging all the food and
conversation." He would whisper this while looking down
the table at Brenda, her mom, and her seven siblings, who
were all chattering away as they ate.

Brenda had secretly dreamed of becoming a comedian for years. She idolized Joan Rivers's self-deprecating
humor and Whoopi Goldberg's prickly perspective. She
imagined that she would be comfortable onstage, but she
never thought she was smart or cute enough.

As Brenda and her friends were enjoying themselves
at the comedy club, Brenda boldly claimed, "I'm going to
do that for my fortieth birthday. You'll see *me* up onstage!"
Her friends laughed and nodded politely. They thought it
was Brenda's jumbo margarita doing the talking.

Brenda worked as a hairstylist, a job she had held
since turning twenty-one. She never thought she would
be a hairstylist. "I just went in for a haircut one day in my

late teens, and the stylist asked me what I was going to do with my life. I didn't know, so he suggested cosmetology. Talk about impressionable!"

Brenda didn't have any money for college, nor did her family. Cosmetology seemed like a reasonable option to make ends meet. Conducting market research over the telephone in high school had also given Brenda some experience in communicating effectively and asking good questions. In beauty school, she had no problem forming personal connections with her clients, but she didn't think she could cut hair very well. She hoped her confidence would improve as her skills did.

Brenda eventually became a very good hairstylist, and people loved talking with her as she cut their hair. She enjoyed listening to their stories, too, and occasionally offered some advice. She also enjoyed soaking up her clients' wisdom.

Life was busy for Brenda. Her husband, Bahgat, worked full-time in the computer industry, and they had two young children, John and Hannah. The biggest drawback of Brenda's job was that she had to be on her feet for long hours. As a result, she suffered badly from hemorrhoids. Sometimes they bled. "I became really good friends with the folks at our local drugstore, always in line with a handful of Tucks containers and Preparation H tubes," Brenda joked.

Shortly after her thirty-ninth birthday celebration at the comedy club, Brenda's hemorrhoids started acting up. It was hard for her to find a comfortable position. The pain was unbearable, and her usual remedies weren't working. One night, she and Bahgat were making love and Brenda had to stop. The pain was excruciating. Sex had never been a problem before.

She saw her family physician the following week. He examined Brenda and thought it was her hemorrhoids. But that day, a general surgeon with experience in surgically treating hemorrhoids was also in the office. Brenda's physician wisely asked him to see her for a second opinion.

The surgeon was "bold, serious, and possessed an air of self-confidence," Brenda remembered. He introduced himself and got right down to business. He examined Brenda, and the pain was like nothing she had ever felt before. Trying to distract herself, Brenda said to the surgeon, "Doctor, why do you think God put our rectums way back there? Why not on our hips or someplace easier to reach?"

Not even a tiny chuckle escaped from the surgeon. He continued his examination, taking biopsies of the large tumor in Brenda's rectum.

Brenda remembered the moment that the surgeon told her she had rectal cancer. "I cried uncontrollably and felt as if my spine was turning into jelly and liquefying into the chair." The surgeon explained to Brenda that she would need to have part of her rectum removed and part of her vagina removed and reconstructed, as well as a complete hysterectomy and a permanent colostomy for the rest of her life. It wasn't clear whether she would also need chemotherapy or radiation. Her life expectancy could be very short, or it might be normal.

As she drove away from the office, sobbing, Brenda planned her funeral in her head. Usually an optimist, Brenda couldn't keep her mind from thinking about all the unknowns: *How will the kids and Bahgat handle my hair falling out? I don't want them to see me throwing up, listlessly lying around with my pajamas on and no energy to lift my babies into my arms. No other woman can mother them the way I do. They like it when I read to them in funny voices and when we pray together at night. I want to see my children grow up, to get excited with Hannah as she dresses for her first Sadie Hawkins dance or see John driving for the first time. The thought of not laughing with them about private jokes or exploring the fifty states together makes me crazy. Bahgat needs teasing; he works too hard and takes life too seriously. I want to visit Paris with him. It took us too long to find each other.*

That night, Brenda, Bahgat, John, and Hannah visited Brenda's parents to share the news. Brenda shared the news with her mom and dad, who compassionately and lovingly listened to the details of the day's events. Brenda asked her dad, Eugene, financial questions. "Dad, do you think Bahgat will have enough money in case I die? I don't even know what kind of life insurance we have on me. I bet it isn't enough." Eugene let Brenda ask all the questions she had. Then he said calmly, "You know Brenda, you just might live."

They laughed, and the tension in the room broke. Brenda hadn't really thought of that possibility yet. Several siblings and relatives soon arrived at the house to hear the news. At one point, there was some commotion, and Brenda's aunt Betty said loudly, "Brenda, did you say you have colon cancer or cancer of the rectum?"

Brenda responded, "The doctor called it colorectal cancer. He said the rectum is the lowest part of the colon.

So, I have cancer of the a—hole!" Everyone laughed.

News of Brenda's diagnosis spread through her social communities. Brenda also learned that her cancer had likely *not* spread beyond her rectum. She continued working and received great support from her coworkers. "Sometimes no words were spoken," Brenda recalled. "One stylist blew me a kiss as she walked by. Another squeezed my hand, while a third paused to give me a hug."

Brenda's friends and family pitched in, from cleaning her house and preparing meals to taking her to appointments and watching John and Hannah. They also helped Brenda keep the mood light. For instance, one of Brenda's sisters, Laurie, who lived abroad in Japan, wrote e-mails, wanting to help. One of them read, "Brenda, I guess I could donate my vagina if you need it. Mine hasn't had much use lately. I prefer to keep my own rectum, however. Love, Laurie."

One of the lightest moments for Brenda in those initial weeks came when she met with the gynecological surgeon to discuss the vaginal reconstruction that would take place during her surgery. The surgeon mentioned that extensive scar tissue would likely result, and that her vagina might close completely. Since Brenda was a young married woman and sexually active, the surgeon said that she might need to wear a dilator inside her vagina to help prevent the walls from healing shut. Without hesitating, Brenda said, "If I have to wear a dilator, I hope at least it vibrates!"

The day of Brenda's surgery arrived. She was nervous. Besides the day she had received her diagnosis, this was the most frightened she had ever felt in her life. What if something went wrong? What if the cancer was more advanced than her tests showed? As the worries built up, Brenda started to feel a lot of anxiety.

Then something unexpected happened. That morning, Brenda's mom, Helen, came to the hospital to see Brenda before she was taken back to the operating room. Helen was the serious one in the family. She didn't laugh very much, if at all, and she was always cleaning, organizing, and keeping the family on task.

"This is for you, Brenda," Helen said, giving her daughter a small box.

"Wow, Mom, a gift?"

It was out of character for Helen to be spontaneous, especially spontaneously generous. Brenda was touched by the gesture. She opened the box to find a beautiful pair of earrings.

"These are stunning, Mom. Thanks."

"There will be another pair waiting for you when you get out of surgery," Helen replied.

Brenda laughed. "Is that a bribe, Mom? I bet the other pair is even better. You're saving them in case I die, aren't you?"

"Oh, Brenda, how can you say that?" Helen laughed.

"Now I have a reason to live, Mom, if the suspense doesn't kill me," Brenda kidded.

Brenda and her mother laughed harder together than they had in quite some time. Then Helen bent down and gently kissed Brenda, giving her a sense of peace that only a mother's love can provide. When she got into the operating room, Brenda told her rectal surgeon, who by now she referred to as "the Rear Admiral," to do a good job. She asked her gynecological surgeon if his hands were steady that day. He replied, "Yep, so far I've had only one cup of coffee."

Seven hours later, Brenda woke up in the surgical intensive care unit. The operation had gone smoothly. She had staples from her chest to her pubic bone and a colostomy on her abdomen. She also had a feeding tube hanging out of her nose, a Foley catheter between her legs, and pneumatic compression stockings on her legs to prevent blood clots.

When Brenda awoke, Bahgat was at her bedside. He leaned in. Brenda knew he would say just the right thing to comfort her.

"Brenda, honey, you look like the back of my stereo system."

Brenda couldn't resist laughing. It hurt to laugh, but it felt really good at the same time. The first physician to visit Brenda after her surgery was the Rear Admiral. "Good news, Brenda," he said. "I'm almost certain I got it all."

Brenda started to cry. "Thank you from the bottom of my heart," she said.

"My pleasure," he replied. "And I'm not sure why God put rectums where they are." They laughed together.

Brenda remained in the hospital for fifteen days, recovering and learning about what she called her "new uniform"—which included a remodeled vagina and a colostomy. Every day, one or two of Brenda's friends visited. Night after night, with a friend at her side, Brenda slowly walked the hallways to gain strength. Brenda's room filled up with cards, flowers, balloons, and other tokens of goodwill. Her brother, Rick, brought the most memorable gift.

"Uh-oh, Rick, what have you got there?" Brenda asked as he entered the room.

"Something from your past that I thought you should have now," Rick said with a wayward grin.

Rick had brought Brenda the four-foot-tall lawn ornament that Brenda had given to him as a joke years before—a plywood lady who was hunched over, revealing her plump buttocks underneath a colorful dress. Across her buttocks, Rick had drawn a big red circle with a red line through it.

When she arrived home, Brenda continued to feel the strong support of her family and friends. She also received the official news that she wouldn't need chemotherapy or radiation. The Rear Admiral had removed all of her cancer, just as he had thought. Perhaps the biggest transition for Brenda was learning how to accept and manage her colostomy. The steep learning curve sometimes discouraged her. It was a radically new normal for Brenda and not one that she was particularly excited about. But she knew it was better than the alternative.

"I felt sad about living with a colostomy, even though I was grateful for life," she remembered. "I tried to laugh as much as I could, even if I had to force it sometimes."

John and Hannah played a big role in Brenda's recovery. "My kids were my chief motivators," Brenda said. She wanted, more than ever before, to be strong for them and to be there for them whenever they needed her. Brenda also started noticing John and Hannah in fresh ways. She watched them with great joy and wonder as they played. She imagined growing old with her children, getting them through childhood and adolescence, and then watching them form their own families and contribute to society. Rectal cancer had forced Brenda to pause and appreciate her kids, Bahgat, and their life together in a whole new light.

One day, a good friend of Brenda's handed her a brochure for Pathways, a health crisis resource center in Minneapolis. The Pathways mission was to help people cope with terminal illnesses or chronic health conditions. Right from the start, Brenda was impressed. "The walls and people oozed of acceptance," she said. "Pathways became a really safe environment for me to openly share my story, grieve, and reflect."

At Pathways, Brenda began a nine-week class called "Renewing Life." She learned to make choices that were better for her. She also learned about the meaning of illness, and how it could move one to find new meaning and purpose. She shared with the other participants that her sense of humor was a big part of how she stayed resilient. She also took advantage of the activities that Pathways offered, including energy balancing, yoga, art, dance, and meditation. Sometimes Brenda felt a little out of place and thought to herself, "This is weird, having people humming over me." But she was always touched by each person's desire to help her, as well as the stories of the other Pathways participants who, like Brenda, had come there bearing the burden of fear.

Here's how Brenda would later describe her experience:

> I resolved to live in the moment whenever possible. Time was precious, and I didn't want to waste a minute of it. I was determined to never spend a

whole day of my life cleaning my house again. My windows would probably need attention, but not more than my daughter or son. Pathways helped me to clarify how I wanted to live the rest of my life, with purpose, choice, and bold announcements of love. I didn't want to live with regrets. Ironically, cancer became a gift of opportunity that enhanced my life.

With a renewed sense of purpose and meaning, and with humor now an even greater part of her story, Brenda knew that she needed to start chasing a big dream, one that had been inside of her for quite some time.

●———●

Charlie Chaplin once said, "To truly laugh, you must be able to take your pain and play with it." Like Brenda, most of the playfully intelligent people I have spoken with for this book use their senses of humor not only to connect with others, but also to cope with stressful situations or experiences. Vivienne and Dan certainly did. In the playfully intelligent mind, humor isn't necessarily called upon for every difficulty that is encountered—it isn't a default coping mechanism, in this sense—but it is something that can be consciously called upon, in various capacities, when needed. That's not to say humor always works (to strengthen a connection or get us through a rough spot). In fact, in many ways, humor is like a medication that only works some of the time. But if you never think about what it *could* do—it will never have a chance *to* do anything.

It's important to note that, in my interviews, I did not observe humor being used as a way to escape or avoid challenges at hand. Brenda fully suffered the painful emotions and grief that came with her rectal cancer journey. She didn't use humor to blow off her reality. She used it as a way to gain a little air and control in a situation that felt very much out of her control.

Humor theorists hypothesize that this is precisely the mechanism through which humor provides us with resiliency. When we are able to laugh or find humor amid stress, we give ourselves a psychological distance from the situation that turns out to be incredibly powerful. By placing ourselves in an observant role, standing beside our pain, we can look at it from a lighter point of view. The key is that this distance is never very far. We aren't running away from our stress. We are standing next to it. We aren't denying the trauma of the adversity itself. We are using humor to improve the emotions and psychology that surround it.

In the laboratory, simulating stressful experiences for study subjects and then measuring their responses has been a popular model used to study the humor-resiliency link. It's somewhat distressing to think about this kind of research actually taking place, with participants usually watching stressful videos, working on unsolvable math problems, or being told (falsely) that they are going to receive a small electric shock. But what has been found is that those participants with higher levels of humor or those who create humor narratives for what they're doing or watching usually experience less stress.

So, how well does the humor-resiliency link hold up in real life, outside the laboratory? Considerable research on this question has been conducted on prisoners of war as well as Nazi concentration camp survivors. One study evaluated crewmembers of the *USS Pueblo* shortly after they were released from a North Korean prison in 1969. Better psychological adjustment was correlated with the use of humor. The prisoners noted that joking about the characteristics of the prison guards, using humorous nicknames for the guards and fellow prisoners, and telling jokes to each other gave them a sense of control. Similarly, in several studies of American prisoners of the North Vietnamese Army, humor was found to be one of the top resiliency traits. Some prisoners noted that they would risk being tortured just to tell a joke through the walls to another prisoner in need.

Perhaps the most notable prisoner to have explored the humor-resiliency connection is Viktor Frankl, an Austrian neurologist and psychiatrist who was also a Nazi concentration camp survivor. In his book *Man's Search for Meaning*, Frankl wrote:

> Humor was another of the soul's weapons in the fight for self-preservation. It is well known that humor, more than anything else in the human makeup, can afford an aloofness and an ability to rise above any situation, even if only for a few seconds.

Thinking about Brenda, coping with the stressor of life-threatening illness, the research evidence on humor's resiliency effect in this situation is less clear. Women suffering from breast cancer have been studied most, and a correlation between humor and resiliency has not been found, with one exception. One study looked at how women who were undergoing treatment for breast cancer interacted with their husbands. It found that women with husbands who gently and respectfully inserted some element of humor into their interactions had lower levels of stress.

Which is perhaps where the real wisdom lies. The notion from the first half of this chapter—that humor is a force that connects us to one another—is quite possibly the essence of its resiliency effect. When humor connects us to another person in times of stress, we feel and experience the support of that person and, in turn, feel more resilient. This parallels the notion of gallows humor, which is humor shared between people who are experiencing suffering together. Gallows humor is common in cancer support groups and has been shown to enhance and strengthen the social bonds that exist within those groups, giving members resiliency.

For Brenda, as for anyone else who has confronted his or her mortality, she never laughed away the fact that rectal cancer could take her life. But she used humor, among other coping strategies, to help balance her sadness. As the saying goes, sometimes life presents us with situations in which we don't know whether to laugh or cry. The lesson is that we shouldn't be afraid to do both. Truvy Jones put it well in *Steel Magnolias*, another 1980s movie, when she said: "Laughter through tears is my favorite emotion."

Vivienne, Dan, and Brenda would certainly agree.

●——●

"Remember, you said you'd do it for your fortieth birthday. You have only six months left!" Brenda's sister, Amy, baited. Encouragement like this as well as her experience at Pathways had provided Brenda with the impetus and confidence she needed to pursue her dream of becoming a comedian.

During her recovery, one of her friends had given Brenda a comedy class as a gift. Now that she was well enough to attend, Brenda was eager to try it out. Her teacher was the late Wild Bill Bauer, a comedy veteran whom Louie Anderson once called "the funniest guy he had ever worked with." Bill encouraged the class members to develop the habit of writing out their material and taught them the art of timing, as well as how to warm up their audiences. Brenda was surprised to discover how much she enjoyed writing down her material, not to mention the challenge of finding the best way to share a new joke.

Her debut came on amateur night at a local comedy club in Minneapolis, two days after her fortieth birthday. Brenda threw herself a party and invited 150 friends and family members. She performed for ten minutes and opened with material on her husband:

> His name is Bahgat. Some people find that difficult to say, so he says, "Call me Baggie." One of my friends calls him "Ziplock."
>
> He had the first stereo surround system I ever saw. Three stereo systems, complete with speakers on three different walls. The only problem he had was finding three friends to push in the

ABBA tapes at exactly the same time.

Bahgat's Muslim. I'm Catholic. We call our children Muslics. They always face east when they say the rosary. They don't eat pork, but they do like to play bingo.

The audience loved Brenda's set. A few weeks later, Wild Bill and several of Brenda's friends encouraged her to enter the Twin Cities Funniest Person amateur contest held at Acme Comedy Club in Minneapolis. Brenda's expectations were low, but to her surprise, she won the first round. And to her even greater surprise, she advanced past the second round. Then, from a field of more than 150 contestants, Brenda found herself in the finals.

After her three-minute routine, she ordered a glass of wine and waited for the judges to announce the winner. "Brenda Elsagher, come on up here; you have won the title of Twin Cities Funniest Person!" Brenda nearly spat out her wine.

The next morning she was on local radio, which was the beginning of a small media blitz. During one interview, a reporter asked her whether she did any public speaking about cancer. Though she had very little experience doing so, Brenda said, "Yes, I do." Then the reporter asked her what she called it. Not having a title in mind, off the cuff Brenda answered, "Humor in Crisis."

Over the ensuing months and years, Brenda would slowly bring her career as a hairstylist to a close and begin her career as a stand-up comedian and cancer speaker. Today, nearly twenty years later, Brenda is a full-time speaker, stand-up comedian, author, and, most important, wife and mother. Most of her talks and writings include tidbits of her cancer journey, especially how humor was a survival tactic for her. For every talk, she starts out by saying to her audience, "Lock eyes with the person next to you and say the word 'rectum' three times really loudly."

Interestingly, when I spoke with Brenda, she reflected back on the day she had received her diagnosis of rectal cancer. She remembered how she had cried continuously. But the second day, she didn't shed a tear. Rather, she laughed about everything. This was when she knew that she needed to laugh *and* cry if she was going to make it emotionally.

She also emphasized that she couldn't have made it through cancer without the support of others, and that humor was and still is a connecting force in her relationships. "People are like gifts you receive," she said. "I collect people and their stories like others collect figurines or baseball cards. The enjoyment I received from being a hairstylist for twenty-seven years is because people and their stories are always revealing and new. We connect through the stories, through the hard moments as well as the funny moments."

In the year following her initial surgery, Brenda and her family traveled to Egypt to visit Bahgat's family. One day, they were sightseeing in a city called Aswan and went to see a set of ancient temples called Abu Simbel, located in a desert on the west bank of the Nile River. On the four-hour bus drive back through the desert, Brenda noticed camel carcasses scattered across the sand. Most were just piles of bones. She started counting them. There were hundreds. Brenda asked Bahgat to ask the bus driver why there were so many of them scattered across the desert. The driver explained:

> The camel farmers of Sudan, the country south of Egypt, bring their camels through the desert to sell them in Aswan. It is a long, arduous journey with no food, water, or transportation for the camels. The physical attributes of the animal equip it to survive hunger and thirst for extended periods of time, even weeks, but sometimes the camel gets tired. Once the camel sits down in the desert, it's almost impossible to get them walking again. Sadly, the farmer has little choice but to leave the immobile camel behind to save the rest of the herd. His livelihood is dependent on keeping the rest moving.

As she gazed out the window at the sand dust stirring underneath the bus tires and the camel bones streaming by, Brenda became emotional. She thought about how cancer or any devastating illness is a vast desert that one tries to get through. She thought about how, like the camel farmers, she had had to leave precious things behind to survive, including parts of her body. For others, that may mean leaving behind a job, a marriage, or a dream.

Whatever it may be for you, remember that humor can be a powerful force of connection and resiliency. When our very existence depends on our relationships and spirit of resiliency to keep us moving through our deserts, this knowledge can help carry us to brighter days.

Humor Well Played

Connection

You can remodel your sense of humor to serve as a connecting force in your relationships by 1) being mindful of the other person's offensive line and 2) showing humility through self-deprecation. Laughing easily and making an effort to spend time doing activities that involve humor— like watching a funny movie or going to a comedy club— will also help.

Practically speaking, imagining another's offensive line and remaining humble will happen in real time, while your interactions with others are playing out. One example of this involves a humorous exchange I once had with my dad. To give you a little background, my dad's first career was in professional hockey. He played for the Pittsburgh Penguins and the Detroit Red Wings in the 1970s. After hanging up his skates, he started a second career in sales, representing various companies that sold collectibles and traveling to stores across Michigan, selling merchandise.

Over the years, my dad has sold just about every knickknack known to the human species, from all varieties of figurines to small lighthouse replicas (Michigan has more lighthouses than any other state). Like Brenda Elsagher, my dad enjoys collecting stories of the storeowners he has met through the years. The relationship dimension of his work has provided him with a sense of purpose and meaning. That said, he would be the first to tell you that he has made a living selling junk. Granted, some of it is good junk, the kind of junk that helps us remember a special time in our lives. But there's been quite a bit of bad junk, too, the kind of junk that clutters our lives.

One Sunday evening, my dad and I went out to pick up some pizza for dinner. He had come to my home earlier in the afternoon to play with my daughters and catch up with me and my wife, Anna. As we were driving, he asked me how my new job was going. I had just accepted a gastroenterology position in a new health system.

"Anth, how's the new job?" he asked.

"Pretty good," I replied. "I like my coworkers a lot."

"Glad you feel good about the change, bud."

"Thanks, Dad."

There was a pause.

"But I don't know how you do it, Anth."

"What do you mean, Dad?"

"You know, the crap you have to deal with, literally, during colonoscopies!"

We laughed.

"Like father, like son, I guess," I replied. "You've had to deal with your fair share of crap and junk, too!"

We both laughed to the point of tears. It was a special moment of connection, built on healthy humor about our respective jobs.

The next time you notice humor making its way into an exchange you're having with someone, remember to imagine where the other person's offensive line is, keep your thoughts humble, and laugh easily. If you do, you'll be well on your way toward a good interaction, one that might even bring you closer to the person you're laughing with.

Resiliency

Finding humor during tough times isn't easy, especially when the situation involves your health or the health of someone close to you. But if you are able to find it, no matter how small, it can be a tremendous source of resiliency.

One way to make it easier to find humor during tough times is to practice finding it during the less tough times. It will be easier to explore your sense of humor as a source of resiliency when the challenge or situation you're facing isn't one of life or death. Then, when something more serious comes along, you'll be ready.

And remember, it's not about deciding whether to laugh *or* cry—it's about choosing to laugh *and* cry.

CHAPTER FOUR

Spontaneity

B ob was born in the 1960s to Mary and Dale Sutherland. With six children close in age, the Sutherlands were a busy family. They lived in a modest
home, tucked away in Royal Oak, a suburb of Detroit,
Michigan. Mary was a teacher and Dale a principal. For
the most part, the two shared house and child-rearing du-
ties. Their parenting philosophy combined being flexible
about certain things and steadfast about other things. As
Bob said, "There were some clear rules and some fuzzy
ones, too."

During the summer, the Sutherlands spent time in the
northern part of Michigan's lower peninsula. The region,
fondly referred to as "Up North" or "Northern Michigan"
by Michiganders, is one of Michigan's best-kept secrets.
Along the northern shorelines of Lake Michigan, wind-
ing sand dunes merge with grand bluffs to form some of
the most beautiful scenery in the United States. Charming towns also abound in northern Michigan, each with
its own collection of ice cream shops, art galleries, and

hole-in-the-wall pizza parlors.

In the late 1960s, the population of southeastern Michigan, where the Sutherlands lived, was growing fast. Mary and Dale knew this and considered the impact it might have on their young family. Having had many positive experiences in northern Michigan, and enticed by its less-crowded space, Mary and Dale decided to leave southeastern Michigan in 1971 and move four hours north to Glen Arbor, a small town nestled on Lake Michigan's northeastern shore.

Mary spearheaded the move. She saw Glen Arbor as a place where her family could grow, play, and be free. As Bob explained, "Mom has always been the family's protector of stress reduction." Mary's father, Paul, influenced her in this sense. In the early 1900s, Paul was a well-known prosecutor in Belmont County, Ohio. Whenever he tried a case, hundreds of spectators would pack the courthouse to watch. Paul leveraged newspaper cartoons and funny stories in his arguments. Weaving comedy into his legal points, he built rapport with the judge and jury while offsetting any stress that had built up. "He had a lot of Matlock in him—colorful, humble, and very fun," Bob said.

Dale took a pay cut when the family moved to Glen Arbor, and he worried about the financial stress it would create; he had been poor growing up. But Mary encouraged him to think about how Glen Arbor would afford them a lower cost of living and more freedom. "Dale, with six children, we will always be poor," Mary told him, "so we might as well be poor and happy!" Her optimism, openness to new experiences, and flexibility had been rubbing off on Dale. As Bob put it, "Mom had a 'Go play!' attitude" that helped Mary live lightly and prioritize unstructured playtime not only for the kids, but also for herself and Dale. It also helped her respect the unpredictability of life.

Once the Sutherlands had settled financially and emotionally into their new surroundings in Glen Arbor, it didn't take long for Dale to pick up where he had left off in Royal Oak, being playful with his children. Bob remembered his dad's dramatic whistling in the morning to wake everyone up. Dale believed that each new day brought new opportunities, and what better way to start things off than cheerful, early-morning whistling? Dale also tried to make it home from school before dinner so he could have an adventure or game with the kids. Capture-the-flag, hiking excursions, and mushroom hunting were his favorites. Ping-Pong tournaments were popular, too—the loser had to do the dishes.

As the kids grew, perhaps the biggest lesson that Mary and Dale tried to impart was that work and fun could coexist. They wanted their kids to see work as something that could have threads of playfulness spun into it. Mary and Dale knew that fun and playfulness could mesh with healthy, productive work, and even make work more beneficial and meaningful.

To encourage this ideal, every summer Dale and the kids worked on a project together. One summer, the family built a wooden deck off the back of their home. From their first trip to Glen Arbor's lumber mill to pounding the last nail, Dale made the project feel like an adventure. He would make up imaginative challenges for the kids, such as finding the right slab of wood at the lumber mill (as if it were a hidden treasure) or pretending that the deck's rails were jail bars that prevented prisoners from escaping. If laughter accompanied the sweat, the summer project was a success.

Another Sutherland work-play tradition was the Petoskey-stone stand. Petoskey stones are made of coral that was formed during the ice ages. As glaciers cut into the coral and bedrock of North America, the stone fragments that broke off became the Petoskey stones that are sprinkled across the northern regions of Michigan's lower peninsula.

Using the business model of a lemonade stand, the Sutherlands would go on Petoskey-stone hunts and then sell the stones that they found for a dime apiece in their front lawn. They put the stones on a card table in small dishes of water because when Petoskey stones are dry, they resemble ordinary limestone. But when they are wet or polished, stunning geometric patterns appear on them. The customers enjoyed the stones and the excitement on the kids' faces. The summer projects and Petoskey stands required work, but fun was always a part of the experiences—exactly as Mary and Dale intended.

As Bob approached his teens, basketball became one of his favorite sports to play. Being athletic and having an outgoing personality, Bob saw basketball as a sport that required a healthy mix of individual talent and team togetherness. By the time he entered high school, Bob stood more than six feet tall, making him one of the tallest kids in his class. At the start of his senior year, he was the star of his high school's varsity basketball team, the Glen

Lake Lakers.

But something traumatic happened during Bob's senior year: Dale was diagnosed with adrenal cancer. Our
adrenal glands produce important hormones that are necessary for survival. Dale had felt tired for several months,
and after an extensive medical evaluation, his cancer was
found. Naturally, the news devastated him, just as it did
Mary, Bob, and his siblings. Adrenal cancer is extremely
rare, occurring in one or two people per million in the
population. On average, only 600 people in the United
States are diagnosed with adrenal cancer each year.

Like most teens, Bob remembered being preoccupied
with himself during his senior year of high school, but he
was also very much aware of his dad's uncertain future.
Dale's cancer, when it was diagnosed, was advanced. His
oncologist gave him less than twelve months to live. This
reality, along with the high expectations to lead his Lakers to a winning season, weighed heavily on Bob's mind.

As his health declined, Dale did everything he could
to attend Bob's games. Bob always heard his dad cheering
from the stands, just as he had always heard Dale's whistling in the morning. Before each game, Dale would tell
Bob, "Remember to have fun out there. Just have fun."
After the game, Dale would tell Bob just how much fun *he*
had had watching his son play.

At the time, Bob didn't think much about his dad's
pregame encouragement. He was just happy to see Dale
in the stands. But looking back, he realized that his dad
was trying to lift some of the pressure off of him as he
trudged through his final year of high school, carrying a
basketball team on his shoulders and watching his father

die at the same time. If one were to ask Dale today about the encouragement he gave Bob back then, he would probably (with a smile) confirm that he wanted to temper some of the pressure Bob was feeling. But then he would likely circle back to the family's summer projects and Petoskey stands for a bigger lesson: fun can be a part of our performances, too, just as it can our work.

Dale passed away when Bob was nineteen years old and a freshman at Northern Michigan University. Although Dale's death was expected, Bob felt a tremendous sense of loss: "I just seemed to lose all of my enthusiasm for life." Remarkably, Bob stayed focused enough to finish his freshman year.

As college progressed, in the spirit of his family's Petoskey stands, Bob began to think about starting a small business. He knew he enjoyed the outdoors and nature. All of Dale's hiking adventures, pretend hunts, and the like had made a big impression on him. So, in his early twenties, Bob started a lawn service company.

The excitement and challenge of running a small business motivated Bob in the beginning. But despite the lesson that Mary and Dale had passed along to their children, Bob had trouble finding the fun in making other people's yards look nice. The money was good, but the work felt monotonous. In hindsight, Bob noted, "It probably wasn't the work, because I think I would have been able to find some fun in it if I had stuck with it. It was probably more that I was still grieving the loss of my dad."

A year after he had opened its doors, Bob closed his lawn service company in search of a better chance at work-play harmony. His first thought was to start a day camp for kids. "I wanted and needed to feel what I had felt when I was a kid, bouncing around northern Michigan with my family." He discussed the idea with a few people and posted some fliers around town. There was some interest, and pretty soon, every morning at ten o'clock, Bob was meeting kids at the sand dunes of Lake Michigan. Over the next five hours, he would serve as the kids' personal Pied Piper, leading them on adventures, just as his mom and dad had done with him and his siblings.

By swimming in lakes, tramping through mud, pushing down dead trees, and hunting for mystical treasures with the kids, Bob started to feel alive again. With each adventure, his enthusiasm for life came back a little more. He rarely had a plan for how the days with the kids would unfold, but that was the point and a big part of his and the kids' fun. "I just stayed open to wherever spontaneity took us," he said.

The day camp's positive momentum transferred to Bob's night job as well. Working as a waiter at the Red Pine diner in Glen Arbor, Bob hammed it up with his customers. "I would deliberately give them back-talk when they were ordering," he said. "If a guy asked for no onions on his burger, I would say, 'Okay, extra onions on your burger, and a side of onion rings, too!'" People enjoyed the back-and-forth, and many customers requested the Pied Piper of Dining upon their return.

"I think the day camp and the Red Pine were opportunities for me to play my way back into life after my dad died," Bob said. "I'll never forget those days and the fun I had with the kids and customers."

Bob was approaching his college graduation, and he

knew that the day camps and Red Pine nightcaps couldn't last forever. He also knew that he never wanted to stop chasing his adult version of the Petoskey stand.

What Bob didn't know, however, was that his next step had been in the making—and growing all around him—for a very long time.

●——●

In the 1800s, Reverend Peter Dougherty, a Presbyterian missionary, was asked by the church's governing body to establish a church and school for the local Ottawa and Chippewa Native Americans, who lived along the northeastern shore of Lake Michigan. Dougherty, a true Presbyterian, worked hard and tirelessly. The natives referred to him as "Little Beaver." He was a perfect fit for the job.

One day, in 1852, Dougherty decided to plant a small cherry orchard near his home. The local farmers and natives told him that the trees wouldn't survive the cold weather, but Dougherty planted the orchard anyway. To everyone's surprise, the orchard not only survived—it flourished. People began to suspect that Dougherty had supernatural farming powers. Soon, every farmer in the region was planting cherry trees and harvesting the fruit. Dougherty had started a northern Michigan cherry revolution.

The farmers and natives came to learn that stone fruit—fruit with a hard pit, such as cherries—needed well-drained soil, since its trees are highly susceptible to rotting in wet conditions. Northern Michigan's sandy soil provided natural drainage for cherry crops. Lake Michigan also helped. In the spring, as the wind flowed west to east across the lake, the air temperature stayed colder longer on the shoreline because it picked up cold air from the lake. This kept cherry buds from blossoming until late spring, when an unexpected frost that could jeopardize a budding crop was less likely.

Today, northern Michigan's cherry production is roughly 250 million pounds of fruit per year, accounting for nearly seventy-five percent of the tart cherries and twenty percent of the sweet cherries grown annually in the United States.

At some point in 1989, Bob Sutherland thought that it might be fun to design a T-shirt and try to sell it. It couldn't be just any T-shirt, though. It had to represent where he had grown up. It had to speak to the soul of northern Michigan and the culture of the people who lived there.

Bob met with local artist Kristin Hurlin, and the two created a concept for the shirt. Several weeks later, the shirts were printed and packed into boxes, which were then loaded into the trunk of Bob's car for him to hawk. That summer, Bob sold a whopping 10,000 T-shirts. He couldn't keep up with the demand. The stores loved them. The locals loved them. The tourists loved them. And Bob was having loads of fun to boot.

But what was so great about the T-shirt?

On the shirt was a beautiful, simple drawing of a cherry tree with little raccoons eating the cherries. Below the tree, vintage letters read, "Life, Liberty, Beaches, and Pie." The shirt evoked a sense of peace, joy, and play in those who saw and wore it.

With some success in his back pocket and a likeable T-shirt in his trunk, Bob, for the first time in his life, realized that he just might be on his way to finding his grown-up Petoskey stand. Strong sales for the T-shirts continued through the summer and into the fall. Bob enjoyed the hustle of getting them into shops, and he liked chatting with the shop owners about how he viewed cherries as an identity for the region. But as winter approached, he knew his T-shirt business would suffer. Who buys a summery T-shirt when it's cold and snowy outside?

Bob began to envision the "ruby-red morsels of joy," as he called Michigan cherries, in a variety of food products that could be produced and sold throughout the year. He met with a few Glen Arbor bakers and described how he wanted to make "a cherry-inspired cookie that would outdo the chocolate-chip cookie." After several recipes were tested, the winner was a moist, round, rolled-oat cookie, with dried cherries and white chocolate chips mixed in. Bob named it the "Cherry Boomchunka Cookie." When deciding on the name, Bob remembers wanting people to feel playful from the moment they purchased the cookies to well after their final bites.

Like the T-shirts, the Boomchunkas were a hit. The same shops that bought Bob's T-shirts also bought his cookies. Over the next several years, spanning the early 1990s, Bob brought his T-shirts and Boomchunkas together under one business roof named Cherry Republic. Many other upbeat, cherry-inspired food products followed the Boomchunka, including cherry salsas, cherry barbecue sauces, chocolate-covered cherries, and cherry trail mixes.

The business grew fast, and Bob made sure that fun always accompanied the work, even if it meant that the work moved a little slower. For instance, in 1995, while Cherry Republic's flagship store was being built on South Lake Street in Glen Arbor, Bob and several employees traveled to Michigan's upper peninsula to find flagstone rocks for the meandering walkways that were planned for the store's grounds. When they arrived at the rock quarry, Bob told everyone to pretend to be either Fred Flintstone or Barney Rubble. As the tractor tossed the flagstone rocks into a pile next to their truck, the team had jumping contests from the quarry's clay cliffs. Whoever performed a creative aerial while yelling "Yabba dabba doo!" the loudest, won.

Over the next fifteen years, Cherry Republic became a staple of northern Michigan's identity and a must-see attraction for vacationers. Today, visitors at the Cherry Republic headquarters in Glen Arbor are met with a sense of joy and playfulness. There are funny, quirky signs everywhere. Bob's mother, Mary, likes the sign that reads: "The owner is a simpleton. Selling more than one fruit would be too complicated for him." Over 200 cherry food products fill the store and the company's mail-order catalog. Cherry Republic frequently holds cherry-stomping, pit-spitting, and pie-eating contests, and it sponsors an annual community talent show, too. Mary likes to dress up as Chiquita Banana to remind everyone that other fruits exist in the world.

As Cherry Republic's chief executive officer, Bob remained agile in his thinking as the company faced and continues to face all the typical challenges that small businesses run into. One such challenge arose in 2012, though it wasn't a typical problem for a small business. In fact, it was the most nerve-racking situation imaginable for Bob, Cherry Republic, and hundreds of Michigan cherry farmers. Normally, Michigan's cherry trees don't blossom until the temperature is consistently warm, which usually happens in early May. But in March of 2012, temperatures across the United States shot up. Many regions of the country logged new record highs. Michigan reached the mid-eighties multiple times—fourteen degrees above its average for that time of the year. The cherry trees started to bud.

Michigan farmer Don Gregory, cofounder of the largest tart cherry operation in North America, put it this way: "When my windows are open and I'm sleeping on top of the blankets in March, I know we're in trouble."

After March's warm temperatures, April went to the other extreme, with northern Michigan recording nearly twenty nights of below-freezing temps. Using a variety of agricultural tricks, farmers like Don scrambled to keep the air warm around their budding cherry orchards. Nothing worked. The freezing temperatures destroyed over ninety percent of the crop.

Don's farm, which usually grew 10 to 15 million pounds of cherries annually, harvested only 100,000 pounds that year. Farms had to lay off workers and also figure out how to manage the operational costs of keeping a farm solvent with no income coming in. As Don said, "It would be like somebody telling you, 'Hey, you're not going to get a paycheck for sixteen months. Now, we expect you to come to work every day, we expect you to pay all your bills, and we'll get you back to a normal paycheck in about sixteen months.'"

Bob and Cherry Republic, being totally dependent on the cherry crop each year, both went into shock. The dreaded nightmare of losing virtually an entire harvest had become a reality. Bob had never thought that something so operationally devastating could actually happen.

Adding to the problem, the cherry surplus inventories were low because of poor crop production over the past several years. With one blow from Mother Nature, the legs of Bob's grown-up Petoskey stand—the cherry trees—had buckled. And his adult Petoskey stones—the cherries—were spiraling downward to the sandy soil, drying up and losing their luster fast.

On an overcast Monday in late April of 2012, Bob called his staff to an emergency meeting at Cherry Republic's flagship store in Glen Arbor. As they gathered in the store's largest room, a somber mood filled the air. The staff knew about the damage. Many employees were already looking for work elsewhere. Bob stood at the front of the room, looking at all the concerned faces. "I wasn't exactly sure what I was going to say," he said. "I didn't have a speech planned."

Taking a deep breath, he began:

> Good afternoon, everyone. I know some of you are off today. Thank you for coming in. I just spent the past weekend talking to some of the cherry farmers. As you probably know, the news isn't good. In fact, it's just about the worst it could be. The crop is essentially gone. Over ninety percent is unusable. I never imagined this would actually

happen, and I don't have a plan B. But I don't
want you to worry. I am going to do everything I
can to keep all of your jobs. You're family to me.
We are going to figure out a way through this.

Bob went home that night and started brainstorming solutions. The next day, he had his plan B. "My biggest thing was to make sure that I put a positive bend
on things," he said. "I thought that if I could find some
playfulness in it all, I might be able to get us to the other
side." Using this strategy, Bob launched what he called
"Operation: Temporary Necessity."

After privately revealing the details of the plan to his
staff, Bob sent an e-mail to nearly 45,000 Cherry Republic customers. It announced that 2012 would be the year
that Cherry Republic called a temporary truce with the
cranberry. To this, Terry Humfeld, executive director of
the Cranberry Institute, responded: "I'm glad there is a
truce, but frankly I wasn't aware there was a war!"

Bob's plan B was to use cranberries as a cherry sub-
stitute. He would also order as many pounds of Lutowka
cherries—which were very similar to Michigan's Mont-
morency tart cherries—as he could from the Lublin region of Poland.

To keep the mood light, Bob hung a gigantic Polish flag in Cherry Republic's Glen Arbor store. Next to
the flag sat a big sign that read: "Long live Poland!" By
mixing cranberries with Polish cherries, and renaming
many products to include the word "cherryberries," Bob
saved his business. In fact, he did more than just save it;
2012 turned out to be a record-breaking year for Cherry

Republic. "Up to that point, we had never sold as much product as we did in 2012," Bob says. What's more, before 2012, specialty crops such as tart cherries had never received federal crop insurance protection. That all changed after Bob's plan B of 2012. Today, farmers of tart cherries and other specialty crops can access federal crop insurance programs to protect them from the whims of Mother Nature.

Bob's psychological flexibility to use cranberries and search abroad for alternative cherry options is what made the difference in 2012. When you really stop to think about it, it makes sense that he was able to quickly adjust his thinking. Bob is a playful and spontaneous guy, and psychological flexibility was a big part of his formative years; he was taught to set both clear-cut rules *and* fuzzier, more flexible rules, to be open to new experiences and adventures, and mesh work with fun.

Bob's Pied Piper nature also nurtures his psychological flexibility. Bob likes to take his employees on day hikes in the summer and play spontaneous games of ice hockey on frozen ponds in the winter. He regularly shows up at the Glen Arbor store unannounced and grabs a few employees for an afternoon excursion. The other employees happily cover the added workload, because they know that their opportunity is next.

In the winter of 2012, after the emotional trauma of the lost cherry crop had begun to subside, Bob threw one of the biggest gala events that the city of Glen Arbor had ever seen. He wanted to bring his community together, as a way of reflecting on and moving forward from what had happened that year. It was a delightful evening of good food, drink, and conversation. People laughed about the cranberries, the Polish cherries, and the Poland flag that Bob had put up.

The guests of honor at the event were the cherry farmers. Bob wanted to give something back to them because he knew they had had it the roughest of anyone that year. The farmers were beyond grateful. "The gala was a night I won't forget, and Bob's generosity will never be forgotten," Don Gregory said. "He has done so much for the northern Michigan cherry industry."

●━━●

When I was growing up, my grandmother would say to me, "Anthony, no matter what the weather is like, move your day forward." Her wisdom usually surfaced when rain threatened an outdoor event of mine, such as a soccer game. In my kid brain, I thought her advice meant that I shouldn't let bad weather spoil my day. Which is true, of course. But as I grew older, her words took on a different meaning.

Those close to me know that I struggle with perfectionism. At times, trying to be perfect has been a great ally, driving me to work hard in school or deliver the best possible care to my patients. At other times, the ugly self-critic that is perfectionism has made it harder to bounce back when things don't go well.

In the beginning of this book, I mentioned that waking up to my life spiraling toward burnout was my inspiration for wanting to explore the power of playfulness in adulthood. The playfulness focus came from noticing how the playful parts of my personality were being usurped by the demands of adult life. In a very real way for me, the work of adulthood—that which is needed for a healthy marriage, effective parenting, and a stable career—seemed to be silencing the playfulness that was inside of me. I responded to this by ratcheting up the perfectness, trying to be nothing short of the ideal husband, father, and physician. But—and fellow recovering perfectionists will relate to this—when a perfectionist has too many things on his or her plate to make perfect, rigidity sets in. Trying to keep every output flawless causes one's spirit to become inflexible. This leads to a fierce irritability that the perfectionist tries to disguise—because the perfectionist can't appear vexed. He or she must always appear happy and unbreakable—these are the hidden creeds of perfectionism. Meanwhile, vulnerability, flexibility, and failure follow closely behind the masquerade that is the perfectionist's life, and their only goal is to be appreciated for what they can offer before it's too late. All in all, a perfect recipe for burnout . . . or at least it was for me.

But here's the upshot.

When I first started exploring what the playful quality of spontaneity truly looked like, I expected to see how spontaneous actions—doing unplanned things outside of routine—led to fun experiences. And I certainly did see this. But as I gathered more data, I also noticed something that I didn't expect to find: spontaneity often reveals itself in our lives as *psychological flexibility*. Essentially, what I was finding and observing in the lives of playfully intelligent people was not only a high regard for spontaneous actions, but also a consistently *flexible* mental response

to the often unplanned and unpredictable nature of life—
such as, say, subbing a cranberry for a cherry.

We traditionally think of spontaneity as something we
can see or experience—a spur-of-the-moment vacation,
or an out-of-the-blue phone call we make to an old friend.
Psychological flexibility, on the other hand, is the spontaneity that we don't always see in front of us. It acts within
our minds every time things don't go as expected. It allows us to mentally ricochet in fresh directions when the
unplanned happens. It eases us through disruptions in
our daily routines and helps us learn how to value them.

My grandmother's advice—to move my day forward
regardless of the weather—was a statement about spontaneous, psychological flexibility. When something happens in our lives that we didn't necessarily think would,
we can either respond in a flexible way or in a rigid, inflexible, perfectionistic way. Since life is full of twists
and turns, the former is much more valuable. It prom-
ises us that, even when something doesn't go exactly as
we had planned or hoped for, we can get through it and
find meaning and contentment. Thinking of psychological flexibility as mini moments of spontaneity inside the
brain has helped me combat the rigidity of perfectionism.

In Chapter 1, we discussed how one can use his or her
imagination to reframe problems. Sometimes being psychologically flexible means imagining different points of
view in a difficult situation. But it can also mean knowing
when to throw reframing out the window and roll with the
punches. What I have found to be true is that the playfully intelligent are adept at this flexibility because they live
in a state where seriousness and intensity don't always

get the upper hand. In other words, there's power in living lightly; psychological flexibility is easier to achieve when one's grip on life is neither too tight nor too loose.

The scientific literature describes psychological flexibility in relation to how one interacts with his or her environment. Adapting to situational demands, rethinking mental resources, changing perspectives, and working with competing desires are all outward expressions of psychological flexibility. Each allows us to make fluid and spontaneous adjustments to the unpredictable nature of the world.

One experiment that demonstrated this involved college students who were living in New York City after the trauma of September 11, 2001. The students were shown a series of pictures designed to stimulate their emotions. The research team then asked one group of students to express what they felt and another to suppress what they felt. Next, students were allowed to choose whether they expressed and/or suppressed their emotions in response to a second set of pictures. When students were given the psychological flexibility (and freedom) to share and/or hold back their emotions, they had better overall adjustment to the trauma of September 11. This experiment contradicted the conventional belief that it's always better to share what one is feeling, and supported the notion that psychological flexibility is perhaps a more useful aim, since it offers a range of problem-solving strategies (including internalizing one's feelings) rather than a select few.

From a neuroscience perspective, the neural circuitry of psychological flexibility likely resides in the brain's subcortical striatum and depends on the functioning of the striatum's cholinergic interneurons (which help the brain change its actions when it faces different stimuli). In one study that supported this neurological geography, researchers damaged the interneurons of rats. The rats' behavioral response to unexpected situations was then observed. In the first experiment, the rats had to press either lever A or B to get a sugar tablet, but only lever A dispensed the reward. Both normal rats and rats with damaged striatal interneurons quickly learned that lever A was the correct lever. When researchers changed the game by flashing a light above the lever that would dispense the sugar tablet, the rats with damaged interneurons had difficulty. The normal rats could flexibly shift their strategy to include the flashing light, but the rats with the damaged interneurons couldn't make the change and continued to press only lever A. Applying these results to humans, the research team hypothesized that since human cholinergic interneurons diminish with age, this may explain why psychological flexibility also declines with advancing age.

Psychological flexibility has been shown to correlate with job performance and satisfaction, mental health, and even pain tolerance. One study that used coldness to produce physical pain found that those with more psychological flexibility could endure the pain longer and experienced a quicker recovery when the cold stimulus was removed. Psychological flexibility is also beneficial when thinking about time orientations. Common wisdom says that one should try to remain in the present and not dwell on the past or live too far in the future. But sometimes it is useful to reminisce about a positive experience from the past. This can improve one's mood and even be a learning tool for the future. Similarly, sometimes thinking ahead toward the future and seeing oneself and one's life down the road is necessary for setting and achieving goals. Having the psychological flexibility to move between past, present, and future time orientations correlates highly with life satisfaction, positive mood, and family and job satisfaction.

Becoming more psychologically flexible takes deliberate effort, however. The first step relates back to Daniel Kahneman's System 1 and System 2 construct that was discussed in Chapter 2. Recall how System 1 aims to solve problems quickly, make judgments quickly, and anchor quickly. System 2 wants to think through the options in a flexible, open, and thorough manner. As you might guess, psychological flexibility requires purposeful activation of System 2, so that one can remain open to different approaches and solutions. This can be challenging, however, because, as we've learned, it's very difficult to change direction once System 1 weighs in.

A good example of this was seen in an experiment that measured people's visual attention level. While counting the number of passes made, participants were asked to watch a video of two basketball teams dribbling and passing the basketball to each other. In one version of the experiment, a woman holding an open umbrella walks the length of the court. In another version, a man in a gorilla suit walks to the center of the court, directly faces the camera, pounds his chest, and walks off. Some sixty-four percent of participants failed to notice the woman with the umbrella. And a remarkable seventy-three percent failed to notice the gorilla! What happened?

For the majority of the participants, the task of counting the number of passes strongly activated System 1 and
deactivated System 2, which would have provided the
psychological flexibility that was needed to notice the
woman and the gorilla. Simply becoming more aware of
how strong System 1 is, in terms of turning off psychological flexibility inside our brains, helps activate System 2.

Let's say you spontaneously decide (System 1) on a
Saturday morning to take a road trip and surprise an old
friend who you haven't seen in years. But you arrive at
his home only to find him out of town. What next? Do
you immediately hit the gas station and begin your return
trip? The answer is no, if System 2 has any say. With a little psychological flexibility, you could instead check out
some of the cultural and recreational opportunities that
the city offers, broadening your horizons and strengthen-
ing your ability to thrive in the unforeseen.

So, if the first step toward greater psychological flexibility is System 1 deactivation and System 2 activation,
ironically, the second step is to not forget about System 1.
How's that for flexibility? In many ways, System 1 is what
allows us to engage in spontaneous activities. Our gut
instincts and impulses, both of which fuel spontaneous
action, come from System 1, as is the courage or nerve to
spontaneously break away from our daily routines. In personality science, this is called "openness to experience."
When one's personality is open to experience, that person
is more likely to be spontaneous in his or her daily life.
With spontaneous activity, one's mind naturally becomes
more psychologically flexible toward and comfortable with

the unknown and unexpected. It's a nifty cycle. System 1 is a spark for spontaneous activity, and while spontaneity is happening, System 2, and the psychological flexibility it affords during the unplanned moments of our lives, is exercised and strengthened.

●━━━●

Lilian Bell was born in Chicago in 1867. Although the U.S. Civil War had ended by the time of Lilian's birth, her upbringing instilled in her a deep empathy for the complexities of war. Many of the men of her family were veterans. Lilian's great-great- grandfather, Captain Thomas Bell, had been an original Virginia patriot of the Revolutionary War. Her grandfather, General Joseph W. Bell, had organized the Thirteenth Illinois Cavalry for the Union Army. Lilian's father, Major William W. Bell, had also gallantly served in the Union Army during the Civil War.

As a young woman, Lilian had a passion for writing and found pleasure in it. At only twenty-six years of age, she published her first novel, *The Love Affairs of an Old Maid*. Reviewers noted her sense of humor and wit. Seven years later, Lilian married Arthur Hoyt Bogue, an event promoter, and the two moved to New York City. Their marriage inspired her to pen *From a Girl's Point of View*, which also drew praise for its wit. By the early 1900s, Lilian had built a strong writing footprint through multiple novels. But as the summer of 1914 wound down, Lilian had no idea that her greatest impact on the world was just on the horizon.

On July 28, 1914, with two shots from a pistol, Yugo-
slavian nationalist Gavrilo Princip assassinated Austria's
Archduke Franz Ferdinand and his wife, Duchess So-
phie Chotek, in Sarajevo, Austria-Hungary. Traveling in
a motorcade, the royal couple was headed into the city
for the day. Ferdinand was in line to become the emper-
or of Austria-Hungary, and Princip believed that killing
him would galvanize Austria-Hungary's South Slav prov-
inces to organize and secede from the Austro-Hungari-
an Empire and form an independent Yugoslav nation.
But instead, the assassination triggered a string of dip-
lomatic crises that led Austria-Hungary to declare war
on Serbia (where Princip and his radical group, Black
Hand, resided). Soon the conflict entangled neighboring
European countries and forced them to side with either
Austria-Hungary or Serbia and declare war on one another. What began as a radical's attempt to gain national
identity had quickly become the start of World War I.

In the beginning, and for the majority of the war, the
United States and President Woodrow Wilson maintained
a position of neutrality. In fact, the United States wouldn't
enter the war until April of 1917, when German subma-
rines began sinking commercial ships, including American ones, that were sailing the North Atlantic toward
Great Britain.

Newspapers were the main source of information
about the war for U.S. citizens. As the war got underway,
the stories being reported were both terrifying and tragic.
Bloody invasions. High casualty rates. Innocent civilian
death. The war was predicted to last only one year—which
wasn't hard to believe, considering the gruesomeness

with which it had begun.

On August 27, 1914, with the war only weeks old, Lilian was sitting peacefully and comfortably in her drawing room. As someone who frequently used her imagination, Lilian allowed herself a few moments to daydream. But unfortunately, her daydream took a wrong turn. She had been reading about the start of the war in the newspapers, and her imagination carried her from her drawing room to war-stricken Europe. She began to experience the horrors that she had been reading about. She found herself hunkered down, face against the dirt and mud of, as she called them, "the sun-baked and water-logged trenches." She started to feel the bodily suffering and mental anguish of the soldiers—"those helpless men, driven out to meet death as best they might," she wrote.

No longer resting peacefully, but balled-up, sweating, and trapped in a daydream turned nightmare, Lilian found her mind drifting to the children of Europe. Surely the children would bring her to a happier place. But rather than dreaming about children joyfully playing, Lilian saw how traumatic the toll of war would be on them and how many of them would become orphans. She herself had never seen her father or grandfathers leave home for the battlefield, but having listened to their stories of war as a child, Lilian could imagine how devastating it must have been for a child to wonder whether his or her father would ever return home.

As her daydream dissolved, Lilian suddenly awakened and jumped to her feet. With clenched hands, she cried out to her empty drawing room, "Oh, God! What can I do to help those helpless ones? What can I do?"

She pictured the coldness of winter approaching, and she thought about Christmas and how on that day, "there would not be a smile on the face of any child in the length and breadth of the devastated land."

Then an idea popped spontaneously into Lilian's mind: "How I wish that I could send a Christmas to all the children in Europe!" But how, and what would it take? With a thundering cry, Lilian blurted out, "A *ship!*" At this moment, she slipped back into her daydream, the good of which was quickly being restored. "The blue walls of my room seemed to fall away and melt into the blue of heaven, and then, under full sail of purple and gold, I saw the ship come sailing."

Lilian began to dream about a ship—a Christmas Ship—setting sail from the United States, overflowing with presents for children, and heading toward the shores of Europe. She saw the grimness on the children's faces changing into smiles as the Christmas Ship arrived, bearing gifts. She imagined adults and military officers of the countries at war pausing to enjoy their first moments free of anxiety since the war began. "I saw the faces of stern warlords relax as the Christmas Ship sailed into their ken." Lilian even pictured the Red Cross helping to distribute the gifts to the European children.

Now awake and inspired, Lilian didn't hesitate, but acted spontaneously on her grand idea of generosity. Her mind immediately bounced to logistics. Where would all the presents come from? How would the presents get to the ship? Where and how would she *get* a ship? Lilian began to think about happy American children playing. What if she could somehow convince the children of America to play Santa Claus for the children of Europe? Her smile broadened. This is it, she thought: the presents would come from the children of the United States—"the work of the children of our land for orphans of war!" she wrote. But how would Lilian rally millions of American children? The answer came to her as fast as the idea itself: newspapers.

The next day, Lilian drafted and delivered a short letter explaining her idea for the Christmas Ship to James Keeley, a friend of hers and chief editor of the *Chicago Herald*. The following day, she received a telegram from Keeley: "Can you get on train and talk over suggestion with me?" Ecstatic, Lilian hopped on the next Chicago-bound train leaving New York City. When she arrived at Keeley's office on August 31, 1914, Keeley said with great enthusiasm, "I haven't been able to sleep since your letter came. It's the biggest thing I have ever heard of in my life!"

Lilian described to Keeley how she planned to call on the generosity of the American children through newspaper columns that she would write, and columns that others would write in other newspapers, encouraging them to put themselves in the shoes of the European children. She explained to Keeley that parents and adults would join the effort willingly once they saw how the children's minds and hearts had been captured by the idea. "Parents will see in the Christmas Ship a new and fascinating way to teach their children lessons of vital importance," she said, "such as the joy of giving, the benefits of self-denial, the sweetness of sympathy, and the dramatic contrast between the horrors of war and the blessedness of peace."

She then explained to Keeley that she planned to move back to Chicago to work on the project.

At the end of their meeting, Keeley asked Lilian to write her first letter to the children of America. "Tomorrow," he said, "I will take it to Washington and read it to President Wilson."

That night, Lilian stayed up to write her letter:

To the Children of America:

When Daddy goes to work each morning you expect him to come home at night. You would be very sad if he did not, wouldn't you? Over in Europe, where kings rule, millions of fathers are being sent to work—the work of war. The kings tell them to go and fight, and they have to go, even if there is no one left at home to earn money to buy food and clothing and pay the rent. Hundreds of thousands of fathers will never come home to their little boys and girls. They will be killed by the fathers of other little boys and girls, who do not really hate them but who kill because they have been ordered to do so.

You will have a Merry Christmas.

Have you stopped to think what is going to happen on Christmas Day to the children of Europe? For these bereaved children there will be no Santa Claus. His sleigh bells will not jingle on the frosty air in the Black Forest, and the snows of the Russian steppes will be untrodden by the good saint's galloping reindeer. Stockings will hang limp and empty in many a French cottage, and the smoky chimneys of England will know him not. No doll for little Jane and no red mittens for Brother John. Oh, what a mockery at this Christmastide!

Children of America, if you could help you would, wouldn't you? And you may!

You can be Santa Claus to those little boys and girls whose daddies died fighting for their country. You can stretch out your hands across the sea bearing messages of love and hope and sympathy to the children of a war-ridden continent—messages from fortunate America to unfortunate Europe.

How can you do all this?

Just in the easiest kind of way, but you've got to do it yourself to get the real joy of it. Earn money to buy the presents, or make them yourself. Every boy knows how to earn money that he may go to the circus. Ask father to let you split the kindling, carry in the coal, carry out the ashes, look after the furnace—and make him pay you for it. Save the pennies that are given to you for candy. Deny yourself something.

And then you ask: "But how can my gift reach the child that needs it?" By the train, and by the boat, and by the train again!

And then you say again: "But the papers say that English ships and French ships and German ships, all armed with cannons, will stop the boat carrying my gift."

They will not! England and France and Germany intend to salute the boat that is carrying your gift—not to stop it. Your ship will be a ship of Good

Will. It will be Santa Claus's ship. And all the countries at war will dip their flags to it as such.

All you have to do is to provide the gifts. Just think what a brave sight the ship will make that carries your gift to Europe. Can't you picture it laden with the thousands upon thousands of presents from the children of America? It will be officered and manned by the fathers of little boys and girls who will take every care that it safely reaches the countries, which are sunk in the want of war.

To Parents: Help your children to learn the lessons of vital importance—the joy of giving, the desirability of self-denial, the sweetness of sympathy, the horrors of war, and the blessedness of peace. This is a worldwide peace movement that will bear fruit—possibly soon, but ultimately, assuredly.

To School Teachers: In all your books can you find a more vital topic? Teach it.

To Clergymen: You have texts galore. Preach this idea—for your Master is the Prince of Peace.

Onward!
Lilian Bell

Lilian delivered her letter to Keeley, who brought it to Washington that week. The response was overwhelming. As Keeley described it: "Washington went wild! I went to see the president and talked as I never talked to any one before in my life. He was sitting there all dressed in white, his face drawn and haggard; but when I explained to him the idea of a Christmas Ship, and he saw how it would make for peace, he buried his face in his hands and tears came into his eyes."

Keeley also spoke with members of the President's cabinet and a number of senators and ambassadors. By the end of his visit, Keeley had secured not only the support of the nation's government, but also that of the USS *Jason*, a 19,250-ton collier that measured 514 feet by 65 feet. The *Jason* was to be Lilian's Christmas Ship.

It took only three weeks for Lilian and Keeley to recruit nearly a hundred of the best newspapers in the country to work on the project. Each newspaper created its own Christmas Ship department, taking its cleverest writers and instructing them to continue generating enthusiasm for the idea. For example, the following was printed in the *Pittsburgh Press* on September 10, 1914:

The sailing of the Christmas Ship will be an act momentous in the history of the world. With an armament of toys and childish gifts, manned with good will and impelled by love, it is likely to sweep all the dreadnaughts and destroyers and death-dealing devices off the seas for all time by rendering them unnecessary. Carrying as it does the Christmas presents sent by the children of the United States to the orphans of war, it seems certain that the recipients of those loving tokens will conceive a warm, deep, and lasting affection for the distant boys and girls who tried to make their Christmas brighter and happier; a firm bond of fraternity which no untoward event of the future could weaken.

Lilian started what she called "Santa Claus Class," a near-daily column in the *Chicago Herald* that included instructions for the children ("keep your gifts small; use your hands to make them") and updates. By the thousands, day schools and Sunday schools across the country began coordinating present-making efforts. The Boy Scouts and Camp Fire Girls of America, as well as adult groups, including hundreds of different women's clubs, the Elks, and the Moose, also began making and collecting presents. Businesses contributed money. Theaters held fundraisers. Even prisoners contributed; Lilian received one letter that read, "From Illinois State Penitentiary, Joliet, Illinois: Enclosed please find one dollar and an abundance of Good Will toward the Christmas Ship fund." Signed, "Thomas J. Bent, Convict 195."

Letters from American children also poured into newspaper offices across the country. Many of them were addressed to Lilian:

Dear Miss Bell,

I am earning money for the Christmas Ship. My mother gives me five cents every time I get 100 in spelling. This is a hard way for me to earn money for spelling is against my nature!

Yours truly,
Ralph

American children also included personal notes with their gifts that were addressed to the European children:

Dear Little Sister Over the Sea,

I hope you will like my dolly. It is the best I've got. I am writing you a letter, which I want you to answer. Tell me about your country and your house, will you? I am sorry your daddy won't come home any more. You poor little thing, I would like to hug you. If you cannot read this, get someone to turn it into your language. If you cannot write English, never mind. Write me in your talk, and I will have someone read it to me in English. Goodbye, dear little sister, and I do hope that the awful war will soon be done.

With love,
Teresa

For Lilian, one of the most touching moments came when a little girl in Minneapolis carried a small bundle wrapped in brown paper to her local newspaper office. Three sides of the package bore the inscription, "For a girl." On the card was a note reading, "From Father."

Although Christianity was the dominant religion in the United States at the time, the work and contributions of people from many different faith backgrounds were represented. Outside of Christianity, the work of the Jewish community was unsurpassed. Some of the most liberal monetary donations for the Christmas Ship came from Jewish merchants.

The spontaneous generosity also reached beyond socioeconomic status. The *San Francisco Chronicle* put it best when describing what was happening in California (which was also happening across the rest of the country): "A great wave of enthusiastic and practical benevolence is sweeping over the golden state of California. All ages, classes, creeds, and national sympathies are being merged in a magnificent effort to express the eternal truth that loving-kindness for little children is the strongest emotion of our common humanity."

All in all, American children donated dolls, teddy bears, sleds, ice skates and roller skates, candy, food, clothing, picture books, toys, games, and much more. When it came time to transport the gifts to the USS *Jason*, most cities used four-horse trucks to carry the gifts to the nearest railroad depots. Then, by means of forty-four different railway systems spanning the country, hundreds of trains delivered the gifts to Bush Terminal in Brooklyn, New York, where the *Jason* was stationed.

When all was said and done, Lilian's Christmas Ship idea generated more than 7 million gifts, valued at over $2 million. What's even more impressive is that of the 100 million people living in the United States at the time, an estimated 40 million helped give the Christmas Ship life—most of whom were women and children. And on top of all this, the whole project took roughly seventy days—less than three months from Lilian's spontaneous first step to November 10, 1914, the day the ship set sail.

The ship's departure day was one of pure elation and celebration. Thousands upon thousands of citizens, soldiers, and Red Cross workers lined the piers and streets. This description appeared in the *Pittsburgh Press* that day:

> Amid the strains of martial music, the shrill blasts of hundreds of whistles, the tolling of bells,

and the shouts of thousands of persons, the USS
Jason—the Christmas Ship—laden with millions
of gifts for the war orphans of Europe, donated
by the children of America, was slowly pulled
away from pier No. 1, Bush Terminal, Brooklyn,
at 12:08 PM today by six tugs, and started down
New York harbor on the first lap of her journey
across the Atlantic Ocean.

Never before in the history of the world has
a ship started across the ocean under similar circumstances and on a similar journey, and its departure was marked with fitting ceremony.

Down the faces of many streamed tears. Wom-
en sobbed aloud, while children wildly cheered
and clapped their hands. A more impressive sight
would be hard to imagine.

The Christmas Ship eventually docked at Falmouth,
England; Marseilles, France; Genoa, Italy; and Salonika,
Greece. From these locations, the Red Cross distribut-
ed gifts to the children across Europe. Children of both
the Allied and Central Powers received presents, since
President Wilson wanted to preserve the United States'
position of neutrality.

Many accounts from leading officials on both sides of
the war reported that the act of generosity caused their
militaries to pause and deeply consider the impact that
the war was having on their countries. For their work, Lilian and Keeley received hundreds of honors from govern-
ments and newspapers all over the world.

World War I ended in 1918, and Lilian Bell died in

1929. By the time of her death, Lilian had nine novels to her name, but she would always consider the sailing of the Christmas Ship to be her greatest accomplishment.

Whenever Lilian was asked about her inspiration for the project, she would simply say, "It came about very suddenly." And indeed it had. In fact, when one accounts for the magnitude of the project, the execution of the Christmas Ship idea happened rather suddenly . . . rather spontaneously, you could say.

Interestingly, when it comes to generosity, science will tell us that this is exactly how it had to happen.

●────●

One common experiment, with multiple variations, that is used to explore questions in economics and other related fields is the "public goods game." In the game, participants receive a set amount of money, or some type of money proxy, such as tokens or chips. Each person is then asked to choose privately how much or how little of his or her money to donate to a community pot. Once everyone has made a decision, the money in the pot is multiplied by a factor between 1 and the number of participants. The resulting total is then divided equally amongst everyone.

In its most basic form, a public goods game can shed light on whether people are more likely to fend for themselves or cooperate. If each person puts all of his or her money into the pot, then each person walks away with significantly more money than what he or she started with. But if one person (or only a few people) puts very little to no money into the pot, then he or she (or they) walks away with significantly more than everyone else. Of course, if everyone just holds on to his or her money, then there is no benefit at all.

David Rand, an economist at Yale University, studies human cooperation, and he uses various public goods games in his research. A question that he has recently studied is whether humans are intuitively selfish or intuitively cooperative. In other words, does a person's gut instinct tend to look out for his or her best interest, or look for cooperative opportunities? A knee-jerk reaction to this question might be that humans are intuitively selfish. This hypothesis draws support from Darwinian principles, under which the fittest, perhaps by definition, must be selfish. But we all know that the human race would not be what or where it is today had it not been for our ability to work together.

To help gain clarity on this question, Rand had to first determine how he would identify intuition. Using Daniel Kahneman's System 1 and System 2 construct, Rand worked under the premise that intuition is fast, automatic, effortless, and emotional. It comes to us quickly and urges us to act quickly, too. Intuition is a System 1-driven process. Conversely, reflection—the opposite of intuition—is slow, deliberate, and nonemotional. It comes to us with time. Reflection is a System 2-driven process. Putting these ideas together, Rand surmised that a decision made quickly is more likely to be driven by intuition than reflection, and vice versa for decisions made more slowly.

To better understand whether human intuition leans toward selfishness or cooperation, Rand designed a public goods game that would measure the speed at which participants decided how much money to put into the pot. If those who made quick decisions gave more compared to those who made slower decisions, this would support the notion that human intuition associates more with cooperation than selfishness.

Rand recruited 212 participants. In his first model, he allowed subjects to take whatever time they needed to make their decisions. He found that those who decided what their contribution would be within ten seconds gave significantly more than those who required more than ten seconds to reach their decisions. Rand then forced participants to make their decisions either quickly or slowly. When participants had to decide quickly, they contributed even more. When participants were forced to decide slowly, they contributed less. To validate his findings, Rand then reanalyzed all his past studies that involved decision time in the context of cooperation. He again found that faster, quicker, more spontaneous decisions were associated with higher rates of cooperation and generosity. He concluded that intuition and System 1 thinking are more strongly associated with cooperation than selfishness.

A real world example of this might be an encounter with a homeless person while walking down the sidewalk. The homeless person has a collection bin and a cardboard sign asking for money. As the walker approaches the homeless person, his or her System 1 might signal something to this effect: "A little money could really help him." But the next set of signals that the walker receives, this time from System 2, says: "He will use the money to buy alcohol and drugs." These System 2 signals dampen the cooperative or generous energy that came from System 1. In other words, according to Rand, generosity is probably the initial, spontaneous urge for most of us, but System 2's reflective power, whether it's accurate or not, can override this.

Here's an even simpler example. Pretend that you are in an elevator, and the doors are open. If you see someone walking toward the elevator from down the hallway, you will likely do nothing. But if the doors start to close or the person starts to run, you will need to make a quick decision about whether to hold the doors open, at a time cost to you, or let them close. You will most likely make an effort to keep the doors open, especially if there is room in the elevator for more people. When you do this, you are exercising spontaneous generosity promoted by System 1 and intuition, on a small scale.

Lilian's Christmas Ship idea came to her very suddenly—spontaneously, in fact. It also came to her when she was using another playful quality, her imagination, to daydream in her drawing room. The Christmas Ship was generosity on the grandest of scales, and, in many ways, spontaneity on the grandest of scales. From the idea's inception to its fruition, the playful quality of spontaneity was critical in ensuring that the Christmas Ship set sail. Those who contributed needed to make decisions quickly, intuitively, and, in this sense, spontaneously. Otherwise, they would have easily been able to talk themselves out of helping via System 2: "This idea is impossible." "There's no way it will work." "It's going to require millions of Americans!" In fact, this is probably exactly what happened in the minds of the Americans who *didn't* help.

Besides the generosity that was spurred through the project's spontaneous spirit, there must have also been a substantial amount of psychological flexibility—the other big way that spontaneity works in our lives. Although there isn't any historical record to this effect, a project as large as the Christmas Ship would have had its fair share of stumbling blocks to overcome by way of psychological flexibility. We do know that, in the years following the ship's departure, Lilian would often note the work-play harmony that was critical to the project's success. "Was there ever a more delightful play-combined-with-work and work-combined-with-play invented than all of us mothers and children sitting down to prepare such a shipload of joy?" she wrote. Work-play harmony, in and of itself, requires psychological flexibility to optimally achieve.

Lilian and her Christmas Ship and Rand's studies all suggest that the playful quality of spontaneity promotes and associates with generosity. This is also in line with spontaneous helping behavior that is seen in very young children, who are almost entirely System 1 intuitive thinkers. It's also exactly what I found to be true in playfully intelligent adults.

Going back to Bob Sutherland and Cherry Republic, Bob's spontaneity reveals itself through both his psychological flexibility *and* his generosity. In addition to the gala event for the cherry farmers at the end of 2012, over the years Cherry Republic has given nearly $600,000 to causes in northern Michigan that preserve the environment, farms, and communities in the region. What's more, anyone who has ever been inside a Cherry Republic store knows that Bob has always offered his customers an abundance of samples. There are usually at least fifteen different products available for sampling. Sure, we all know the social psychology of samples (they translate into sales). But Bob doesn't see it that way. "Yeah, I know the psychology," he says. "But I also know that I want to give my customers a little lift in their days."

One recent symbol of Bob and Cherry Republic's generosity is the playground that was built in the middle of the newest store in Traverse City, Michigan. The playground is a big sandbox that is filled with clean cherry pits (instead of sand) and a large tree that kids can climb. The tree also has a fort that kids can play in. Bob remembers how he and his staff worried about the playground when the idea was being considered. "There were concerns that it would take up too much space, and that it would be hard to keep the cherry pits in the box." But Bob and his staff moved forward because it was a way to give something to the children who visited the store. It also represented the spirit of playfulness that Bob and Cherry Republic want to show their customers.

So, if the playful quality of spontaneity promotes generosity, what does science say about how generosity affects our lives? If one were to become more in tune with spontaneity in his or her life and perhaps in turn discover new generosity, how might this generosity benefit him or her?

Christian Smith, a professor of sociology at Notre Dame University, has researched generosity perhaps more than anyone else in the world. In 2010, he and his colleagues surveyed nearly 2,000 Americans in what was called the "Science of Generosity Survey." It was the largest survey of its kind. Both quantitative and qualitative data were collected.

The first question that Smith and his team asked was whether generosity promotes well-being. They looked at various forms of generosity, such as financial, volunteering, and relational generosity (giving time and energy, in a helping way, to those with whom one has a relationship; neighborly generosity was also studied). Then they correlated generosity with various measures of well-being. Across the board, generosity toward others, of any kind, was associated with greater happiness, physical health, mental health, and a sense of purpose in life. But then the team asked whether this simply represented the notion that people with greater well-being are more likely to be generous—a chicken-or-the-egg scenario.

They found that the arrow probably goes both ways. Greater well-being promotes greater generosity, but generosity also fosters greater well-being. As Smith and his team put it, "It is not just that generosity is caused by some greater original well-being. The well-being itself is also caused in part by practices of greater generosity. In multiple, complex, and interacting ways, bodies, brains, spirits, minds, and social relationships are stimulated, connected, and energized by generous practices in ways that are good for people."

Interestingly, many of the people who were classified as generous in the Science of Generosity Survey regularly practiced random acts of kindness, which, at their core, are acts of spontaneity. Smith and his team asserted that, for generosity to become a sustainable part of one's lifestyle, it must be practiced and repeated. Spontaneity is probably similar.

The next big question on the survey was whether or not Americans are generous. The answer: not really. Only 2.7 percent of Americans give at least 10 percent of their financial income, and 86 percent give less than 2 percent of their income. Making more money was not associated with higher rates of giving. The team also found that only 25 percent of Americans volunteer to some extent in any given year. Smith's conclusion was that "Americans have not 'topped out' their capacity to live in the kind of generous ways that we expect could increase their happiness, health, purpose, mental health, and growth. Only a minority of Americans is living clearly generous lives, however you measure it."

For an interesting thought experiment, consider what Lilian's Christmas Ship idea would look like today, a hundred years later. Based on the Science of Generosity Survey, it would have a very hard time setting sail.

Why aren't Americans living more generous lives? A logical answer is that when Smith and his team conducted the survey in 2010, the United States was in the midst of one of its greatest economic downturns ever. In this sense, when the data were being collected, generosity was probably not a major facet of anyone's life. Another answer is that, as Americans, we have a strong tendency toward individualism, which can often work against generosity. We desperately hold on to what is ours at all costs, because we believe that only those resources can move our agendas and our families forward in the future.

Another part of the explanation may relate back to spontaneity and adult playfulness as a whole. When

our adult responsibilities increase, it takes work and a
heightened level of consciousness to ensure that the playful parts of our personalities don't fall by the wayside in
our crazy-busy lives. Spontaneity is the playful quality
that gets slammed hard in this regard because, as our
lives become more hectic, we become more mechanized,
scheduled, and tied to our routines. We hold on tighter
and fight for inches of control. This is often about surviving the day-to-day, of course. But if we don't lose sight of
how spontaneity—whether it manifests as psychological
flexibility or generosity—can move us into better mindsets and improved well-being, we can position ourselves
to find little pockets of joy amid the crazy-busy days.

•———•

George White was an American theatrical producer and
director who worked in New York City and on Broadway in
the early 1900s. In 1919, the year after World War I ended, White opened a revue called *George White's Scandals*
that featured singing, dancing, and comedy. Its Broadway
run lasted more than fifteen years, and audiences loved
the lighthearted nature of the show.

In 1931, Ethel Merman, a popular Broadway actress
and singer, sometimes referred to as "the undisputed
First Lady of the musical comedy stage," performed in
White's *Scandals*. One night, Merman debuted a song,
written by Louis Brownstein and composed by Ray Henderson, titled "Life Is Just a Bowl of Cherries." The song
and its lyrics, such as "Don't take it serious" and "Live
and laugh . . . laugh and love," encouraged a life that

refused to let worry run amok.

Over time, the song's name has become a popular saying in the American lexicon, but probably not in the way that Brownstein and Henderson would have guessed. Rather than stirring feelings and attitudes of a lighter life—to which the song alludes—today the phrase is used for a mild sarcastic effect when something in life *isn't* going well or according to plan.

We all know that life is never just a bowl of nicely arranged and inviting cherries. It's never a series of perfectly planned moments. Life is messy and complicated and often unpredictable. If anything, life is probably more accurately depicted as the cherry that *doesn't* make it into the bowl. The imperfect one, the one that may not have developed the way that it was supposed to, or the one that has been bruised somewhere along its way.

But here's the thing. The playful quality of spontaneity can make the bumps of life a little bit smoother. By nudging us toward psychological flexibility, and moving us off the road of self-absorption and onto the thoroughfare of generosity, spontaneity becomes an indispensable force in our lives. It transforms the imperfect, bruised cherry that sits outside of the bowl into a delicious pie or a jar of jam—that can be walked across the street to a neighbor, or even carried on a ship to neighbors overseas.

Printed on almost all of Cherry Republic's products is the slogan that first appeared on Bob's T-shirts long ago: Life, Liberty, Beaches, and Pie. For Bob, the slogan is a constant reminder of the guiding principles that he wants to follow in his life. It also reminds him of when he first realized that the adult version of his childhood Petoskey stand was upon him.

"Life" in this case means local life—where you are, the community you live in, and the people who surround you. It is the notion that contentment is found in the near and small. "Liberty" is the freedom to be spontaneous. For Cherry Republic's staff, it means touching the heart of every customer who walks through the door. It's empowering the cherry soda server to be able to spontaneously leave the soda bar to play hide-and-go-seek with a little girl in the store while the girl's parents sample some cherry-flavored wine. It's the staff member serving ice cream who spontaneously whips up a banana split that isn't on the menu, just to brighten a customer's day. "Beaches" represents the importance of playfulness in one's life. And "Pie" signifies generosity. What could be more emblematic of generosity than a freshly baked pie?

One day I asked Bob what his favorite Cherry Republic product is. "Well, it doesn't sell very well," he began. "It's a kind of fancy Rice Krispies treat on a stick. It's crisp rice cereal and crunchy Chinese noodles, with peanut butter, dark chocolate chunks, dried cherries, and miniature marshmallows."

"It sounds delicious," I said. "Why is it your favorite?"

"The stick," Bob replied.

"The stick?"

"Yeah, it's a real twig from a cherry tree. You can even toss it in the woods when you're done. I remember the day the Food and Drug Administration came into the store to tell me that I couldn't use real sticks. I kindly asked them what it would take to be able to use them. They told me that I'd have to sanitize the sticks, bake them, soak them, and do a bunch of other things before I could use them. So that's what we do, and the staff makes the whole process a lot of fun. It all worked out."

"That's really cool. What do you call it?" I asked.

Bob took a moment before answering. Then, smiling, he replied: "Cherry *Wonder*bar."

Spontaneity Well Played

Finding Flexibility

In the exact moment that something in our lives, big or small, doesn't go just as we had planned or predicted, the playful quality of spontaneity has the opportunity to manifest as psychological flexibility within our minds. As we practice being psychologically flexible during these moments, we improve our psychological flexibility over time, becoming better at spontaneously moving our thinking in fresh and productive directions as the unpredictable happens. Here are two ways that you can start playfully improving your psychological flexibility right now:

1. **Break routines routinely.** Humans are creatures of habit. We love our ruts and routines, and for the most part, they help us manage and stay on top of our adult responsibilities. But when we become too closely tied to our schedules and routines, we risk becoming numb. Adding tidbits of spontaneity to our routines can help protect us from going through the motions, emotionless. Spontaneous actions also help build our psychological flexibility because when we are engaging in spontaneous activity, we are venturing into the unknown, which demands a mindset that is flexible and open.

Here are some ideas to break up your daily routine: change the order of your morning ritual; get dressed with your eyes closed; use your opposite hand to brush your teeth; take a five-minute break in your workday to explore, on foot, a part of your workplace that you haven't been to recently or have never been to before; eat one new food or a food that you haven't eaten in a while (cherries?); take a different route home from work; sit in a new spot at the dinner table; or have a spontaneous Saturday—get in the car with no plans and just start driving somewhere (pack an overnight bag to make it more interesting—keep it light!).

2. **Hold emotions lightly.** When a difficult or unexpected situation arises in life, we often experience a flood of emotions and feelings. This flood comes from System 1 activation. We need to feel and experience the emotions that are flowing inside us, but we also don't want to let them overwhelm us. The key to surviving the flood is to hold on to our emotions lightly. When we do this, we deactivate System 1 and open ourselves to System 2 activation—the spark for psychological flexibility.

But how does one lightly hold on to his or her emotions? It's not easy. Some things to try are saying the emotions aloud or writing them down. Another trick is to have a silly code word (I like "ninja") that you can say aloud to yourself when your emotions are getting the best of you. Because you are conscious of what is happening when you say the code word, your brain will naturally move toward System 2 activation and psychological flexibility. One word of caution

here: sometimes you'll have to say the code word multiple times—so make it respectable in case you're saying it aloud when others are around!

The Generosity Hurdle

It was a cold Saturday morning in early April. I was twelve
years old, and school had just let out for spring break re-
cess the day before.

I made my way to the bathroom across from my bed-
room and, with sleepy eyes, gazed through the shutters
of the bathroom window overlooking my neighborhood.
Slowly scanning from one end of the neighborhood to the
other, I noticed that the garage doors of my neighborhood
friends' homes were closed. Jeff and Greg were headed to
Disney World. Kenny was flying to California. Joey and
Tommy were going to Mammoth Cave. Mike would be
someplace warm, but he didn't know the name of it.

I raced out of the bathroom. "Mom, why aren't we going anywhere over spring break? This is so unfair!"

"We are going somewhere, Anthony," my mom replied
calmly. "Today, in fact. So get dressed and eat breakfast.
We will leave in about an hour."

"Where are we going?" I asked.

"It's a surprise," my mom said.

I got dressed, ate breakfast, and then begrudgingly
made my way to the car, where my mom was waiting in the
driver's seat. I was quite sour. I knew the surprise wasn't
going to be a vacation, because I didn't have my suitcase,
and neither did my mom. My sister and dad were also still
in the basement watching Saturday morning cartoons!

For the whole drive, I complained about how my neighborhood pals were going on vacations. My mom listened patiently. After about forty minutes, she pulled into a small parking lot in front of a rundown industrial building.

"Here we are, Anthony," she said. "This is the Baldwin Soup Kitchen."

"The Baldwin Soup Kitchen?" I was puzzled.

"Yes, it's a place where homeless people can come for a warm meal and shelter from the cold. Today, we are volunteering here."

I don't remember my exact feelings as my mom said this to me in the parking lot. I probably wasn't very happy. But when we walked into the soup kitchen and I saw for the first time what poverty looked like, sadness came over me—and the anger that I had been feeling faded away.

It was nearing lunchtime. Earlier in the week, my mom had told the Baldwin staff that we'd be coming. We hung our coats in a small closet and then joined the other volunteers in the serving line. Hot dogs, baked beans, watermelon, sweet tea, and chocolate cupcakes were on the menu.

As lunch drew to a close, my mom and I headed to a room in the back of the building with several of the other volunteers. Easter was the next day, and the Baldwin Soup Kitchen was going to deliver hundreds of Easter baskets to needy children in the community later that afternoon. A large truck had backed up to the loading dock of the soup kitchen, which was around the corner from the room we were in. One of the volunteers asked me if I could jump in and out of the truck to transfer the Easter baskets from the room to the truck. So for the next hour, I leapt in and out of the truck, loading the Easter baskets for delivery.

On our way home that day, I thanked my mom for taking me to the soup kitchen. The experience was the first glimpse of poverty *and* generosity that I had seen in my young life. Since then, I have learned that for one to truly live generously, he or she must overcome what I call the "generosity hurdle" (I call it this in honor of my hurdling in and out of the truck at the Baldwin Soup Kitchen). The hurdle is essentially being able to give without expecting anything in return. In other words, generosity should be unconditional.

The next time an opportunity for generosity presents itself to you, make a genuine effort to look at the situation selflessly, without any expectations for a return on your investment. Then experiment with making a quicker, more spontaneous decision about getting involved. Following these two simple steps will go a long way toward playfully making your life a more generous one.

CHAPTER FIVE

Wonder

Lisa and Brian Dover first met in the parking lot of a mall in Ann Arbor, Michigan. It was a Friday afternoon in late January of 1996. They were undergraduate students at the University of Michigan. Brian's fraternity was hosting its winter formal in Toronto that weekend, and from the parking lot, the fraternity brothers and their dates planned on carpooling to Canada.

Brian had grown up in Monroe, Michigan, a small city just south of Detroit. Lisa was from Fort Lee, New Jersey, which sits across the Hudson River from New York City. Midwesterners at the University of Michigan often have spirited stereotypes of students who hail from the East Coast, and Brian was no exception. "East Coasters are tough and have lots of bravado, which is good. But they can really be a pain sometimes!" he joked. Lisa was actually Brian's friend's date for the weekend. When Brian learned that Lisa was from New Jersey, he facetiously said, "Oh . . . great!"

Lisa and Brian exchanged hellos in the parking lot

and then drove in separate cars to Toronto. The following evening, they found themselves randomly sitting next
to each other at dinner. The Midwestern boy and Jersey
girl quickly discovered that their senses of humor and
interests were similar. Talking more to each other than
their respective dates, Brian marveled at Lisa's beauty
and spunk, while Lisa was taken by Brian's handsome-
ness and wit. At the end of the night, Lisa and Brian were
on the dance floor together. Macarena fever was sweeping
the world, and Brian had everyone, including Lisa, learning the moves and laughing hysterically.

On the drive back to Ann Arbor, Lisa couldn't stop
thinking about Brian, and Brian couldn't stop dreaming
about Lisa. When Lisa's close friend asked her how the
weekend had gone, Lisa responded, "I think I met the
guy I'm going to marry!" The following weekend, Lisa and
Brian were together on the dance floor again at a campus
party. They picked up right where they'd left off in Toronto—joking and laughing, but having serious moments,
too. At one point, Brian leaned in and kissed Lisa. "It was
as if we were the only two people at the party," Brian said.

Brian walked Lisa back to her sorority house. As they
came upon a small puddle on the sidewalk, he picked
Lisa up, lifted her over the puddle, and then gently lowered her to dry ground. "Time stopped for me right then,"
Lisa remembered. The two kissed in front of Lisa's sorority house and then said goodnight, knowing that they were
falling for each other.

As college continued, Lisa and Brian's love continued to grow stronger. On February 22, 2000, Brian picked
Lisa up at her apartment for a dinner date. By this time,

Lisa was in graduate school at the University of Michigan School of Social Work. Brian had just completed his undergraduate degree in economics and was preparing for his first job as a financial analyst with Goldman Sachs in Chicago.

Brian bought an outfit for Lisa to wear that evening—a lavender top, black skirt, and tall black boots. They enjoyed a delicious meal at a local seafood restaurant in downtown Ann Arbor. The weather was unseasonably warm that night, so after dinner they strolled through campus, reminiscing about all they had been through together. At one point, Brian noticed a puddle on the sidewalk. As he had done four years before, he picked Lisa up and lifted her over it. But this time, after he lowered Lisa to the ground, he also lowered himself to the ground.

On one knee and with a ring in his hand, he said to Lisa, "I can't go to Chicago without you. You give me more confidence than you can imagine, and I want you to be more than just my girlfriend. Will you marry me?"

Lisa excitedly accepted Brian's proposal, and the college sweethearts moved to Chicago in May of 2000. Lisa landed a social work position in the Windy City, and Brian settled into his role at Goldman Sachs. When they weren't working, they planned their wedding or goofed around together. They enjoyed rollerblading on the lakefront and exploring Chicago's restaurants.

On May 26, 2001, Lisa and Brian got married in Fort Lee, New Jersey. It was a traditional Italian wedding, celebrating not only Lisa and Brian, but also the heritage of Lisa's mom and dad. The day was cloudy with a light rain. But as Lisa and Brian were saying their vows, the sun came out and shone delicately through the stained glass windows of the church. That night, they danced the night away, just as they had many times before.

After their wedding and honeymoon, Lisa and Brian continued to enjoy everything Chicago had to offer. However, a real estate venture in Brian's hometown of Monroe, Michigan, and a social work opportunity in a nearby school system brought the newlyweds back to Michigan. Brian settled into a real estate management role and also started building his own financial services business, while Lisa found her calling in the public school system, working with young children.

Shortly after their move back to Michigan, Lisa and Brian began to think about expanding their family. They didn't have any problems becoming pregnant. In fact, they were successful in their first month of trying. From that day forward, they did all the things that expectant parents do. Lisa read the pregnancy books, and Brian pretended to read them. The prenatal tests and ultrasounds were all reassuring. They gave their parents a framed ultrasound picture of the baby—it was a girl! In both families, she would be the first grandchild of their generation. Brian built a nursery—pink with white crown molding.

Around 4:00 AM on December 29, 2005, Lisa jostled Brian awake. Her water had broken. Later that morning, Lisa and Brian's baby girl arrived. She weighed five pounds fifteen ounces, and was just over nineteen inches long. She was one month early and tiny, but she passed all her newborn tests with flying colors. Lisa and Brian were overwhelmed with joy. They named their new baby Ella Rose.

Lisa, Brian, and Ella arrived home from the hospital to the love and support of both their families. Everyone wanted to hold Ella and have a picture or two or three with her. Ella's new grandparents helped cook meals, do laundry, and keep the house tidy and clean. "It was perfect," Brian recalled.

But within several weeks of being home, Lisa began to have postpartum anxiety. Her biggest fear was that she wouldn't do everything perfectly. She felt nervous holding Ella and didn't want to leave the house. Lisa's primary care physician prescribed some antianxiety medicine, which helped, but it didn't completely relieve her symptoms.

Ella was also starting to fall behind on her physical milestones. Socially, she was smiling and giggling as expected, but physically, she wasn't where she needed to be. At three months old, she couldn't raise or control her head with any consistency. She was also having trouble grasping objects and wasn't swiping for them when they were dangled in front of her. Ella's pediatrician thought that maybe her development was slow because she had been born early. Lisa blamed herself. Maybe she hadn't held Ella or repositioned her often enough.

Ella began twice-weekly physical therapy sessions. At six months old, her head control and core strength began to improve, albeit slowly. At Ella's nine-month checkup, she could sit unassisted. But when Ella approached her first birthday with persistent core muscle weakness, Lisa's concern grew. She talked to Ella's pediatrician, and the decision was made to get an MRI of Ella's brain.

About a week after Ella had her MRI, the telephone

rang. Lisa was sitting in her office at school. It was the pediatric neurologist who had looked at Ella's MRI films. "There is a finding on Ella's MRI that I want to speak with you about," the neurologist said. Lisa could feel her heart starting to speed up. "Ella has a condition called subcortical band heterotopia, or double-cortex syndrome. It's very rare. She will likely have developmental delay. In the worst-case scenario, she may develop treatment-resistant epilepsy, with uncontrollable seizures."

The neurologist continued to talk, but Lisa had stopped listening. Her dreams of a bright future for Ella began to fade. Ella wouldn't be a normal kid. Lisa started shaking and crying.

Brian was equally devastated. He had been thinking earlier in the week about starting a college savings account for Ella; now, he feared she wouldn't need one. Lisa and Brian tried to learn everything they could about subcortical band heterotopia. It occurred during embryonic development, when brain cells mistakenly migrated to areas of the brain where they weren't supposed to be. The out-of-place cells disrupted normal brain function. Symptoms could vary widely, from normal intelligence, no seizures, and few physical limitations to severe cognitive disability and intractable seizures.

The good news was that Ella seemed to be progressing well with her physical therapy. Her social development was also moving forward, with more smiling, giggling, and appropriate interactions with others. Kids gravitated toward Ella's animated persona. They were drawn to the warmth of Ella's eyes and her funny facial expressions.

Ella began occupational and speech therapy, along

with her physical therapy. The plan was to treat any functional limitations early and often, in hopes of preventing them from worsening later. For several months, the strategy seemed to be working. Ella continued to catch people's eyes. "She was the center of attention everywhere we went," Lisa said. Ella also seemed to be helping Lisa and Brian survive. "The best medicine for Ella was Ella," Brian said. "We couldn't stay sad when we were with her because she's so funny and lively."

What's more, and perhaps most important, Ella slowly began to reset Lisa and Brian's senses of wonder. The smallest of progress that Ella made—like purposeful movements or sounds resembling words—created deep, inspiring sensations of wonder and awe inside of them.

Lisa and Brian hoped that as long as Ella kept up with therapy, everything would be fine. But on October 4, 2008, several months shy of Ella's third birthday, things took a turn for the worse. Lisa was having lunch at a restaurant with Ella and suddenly noticed that Ella's eyelids were fluttering. Lisa tried to get Ella's attention by saying her name. Nothing. She said her name louder and then shook her daughter's arm. Still nothing. She couldn't get Ella back. The spell lasted about ninety seconds. Then it happened again. Lisa called Brian. "I think Ella is seizing," she said frantically. "We need to take her to the emergency room!"

When they arrived at the hospital, the neurology team quickly covered Ella's head with electrodes that were connected to wires leading to a computer. Seeing Ella "wired up," as Lisa and Brian called it, for her first electroencephalogram (EEG) was heart-wrenching. It was as if each electrode represented a lost dream: Ella wasn't going to be a normal kid. Ella might never fall in love. Ella would never go to college.

Seventeen more seizures ravaged Ella's brain that day, and for the next six months, despite an unthinkable number of different anticonvulsant medications, her tiny body endured forty to eighty seizures a day. The seizures could happen at any moment, ranging from a small head-bob or series of eyelid flutters to full-body shaking. Sometimes Ella's arms and legs would flail wildly and uncontrollably, and her lips would momentarily turn blue. Lisa and Brian wondered how long Ella could survive like this.

The seizures erased the motor progress Ella had made in therapy. They also deleted the wonderful and at times mystical part of Ella's personality. The facial expressions, smiles, and giggles were gone. Ella's medical team kept making small dosage adjustments to her medications, but nothing worked. Lisa and Brian, as well as those who were helping them at home, tracked Ella's seizures in a logbook each day to see whether any of the medication combinations were working. The only pattern they found was that Ella's seizures had no pattern. And they were not only stealing everything about Ella away, but also—with each head-bob, flutter, twitch, jerk, or shake—shredding to pieces any hope that Lisa and Brian had for Ella's recovery.

●———●

Before the advent of modern medicine and scientific inquiry, healers and physicians sporadically and haphazardly used different concoctions of chemicals and substances to treat illness. Sometimes they got lucky, and their potions worked. But more often than not, patients succumbed to their diseases. Different diets were also tried. These usually failed, too, with the exception of one clinical scenario: fasting and seizures.

For thousands of years, fasting and starvation techniques have been explored in the treatment of epileptic seizures. In 1921, Rawle Geyelin, a prominent New York pediatrician, provided the first report in the medical community on the successful treatment of severe epilepsy by fasting.

Hugh Conklin, an osteopathic physician practicing in Battle Creek, Michigan, had actually prescribed the fasting treatment, and Geyelin, using his connections within the medical establishment, presented Conklin's results. The case involved a ten-year-old boy who "for four years had grand mal and petite mal attacks which had become practically continuous." After the second day of a fifteen-day fast, "the epileptic attacks ceased, and the child had no attacks in the ensuing year."

Geyelin's report amazed neurologists and patients all over the world. At the time, phenobarbital and bromide chemicals, both carrying significant side effects, were the only available treatments for epilepsy. Conklin's experience, as well as subsequent reports that documented similar results, set off a flurry of epilepsy research.

Along with the renewed fervor for epilepsy research came an equally high interest in metabolism and diabetes. Researchers were discovering how insulin allows glucose from carbohydrate metabolism to be taken up by the body's cells and used as fuel for cellular processes. In the absence of insulin, or when cells aren't responding to insulin, as in Type I and Type II diabetes, respectively, researchers were learning that the body draws on its backup energy source: fat.

The problem that was being unveiled through the research was that fat metabolism is messy. When the body breaks fat down, a residue is left behind in the blood, called "ketone bodies." If the level of ketone bodies in the blood is too high, the body goes into an acidotic state called "ketoacidosis." Cells stop functioning optimally, and this can lead to coma and even death.

Fasting, in which few to no carbohydrates are consumed, causes a similar state to diabetes. Fat in the patient's body becomes the primary fuel source for cells, and ketone bodies are produced as a byproduct of fat metabolism. As long as diabetes isn't present, there is usually enough stored glucose in the body to prevent ketoacidosis.

Epilepsy researchers thought that maybe the ketone bodies in fasting epileptics were somehow dampening neuronal activation and, in turn, eliminating seizures. Knowing, however, that patients couldn't just fast forever, they wondered whether a diet that consisted of ultra-high fat, low carbohydrate, and low protein could simulate a fasting state.

In 1924, this exact diet, now known as the "ketogenic diet," was introduced as a treatment for severe epilepsy. The results were staggering. Patients, especially children, with a history of refractory seizures became seizure-free. The ketogenic diet was considered a monumental scientific achievement, and it quickly became a staple of epilepsy management in the 1930s. It wasn't perfect and didn't work for every patient, but it was a welcome alternative to the toxic anticonvulsant medications that were available at the time. In 1939, Dilantin, a new anticonvulsant medication with much fewer side effects, was discovered. Dilantin spurred another era of epilepsy research, but this one was dominated by drug development. New anticonvulsant medications with less side effects came on the market, and the ketogenic diet and other epileptic diet strategies lost momentum.

In the early 1990s, more than a half-century later, a two-year-old boy named Charlie Abrahams developed violent seizures that were refractory to anticonvulsant medication. His father, Jim, began searching for treatments on his own and found references to a high-fat diet that had been used many years ago. Jim brought Charlie to Johns Hopkins University, where the ketogenic diet was still occasionally being used to treat severe cases of epilepsy.

Within several days of starting the diet, Charlie's seizures lessened, and soon disappeared altogether. Charlie remained seizure-free for the next two years, and Jim, a filmmaker and philanthropist, used his talents and connections to spread awareness about the ketogenic diet. This spawned modern-day research on the diet and sparked renewed interest in it as an epilepsy treatment option.

During the winter of 2008, the darkest time of Ella Dover's young life thus far, Lisa and Brian discovered the miracle of the ketogenic diet. They received a Christmas card from one of their friends who had a young boy with Doose syndrome—a milder form of epilepsy—that mentioned how their son had become seizure-free after starting the ketogenic diet. Lisa and Brian had heard of the diet before, but had been wary of restricting their life even more. Now, at their friend's prompting, they decided to give it a try.

The ketogenic diet must be administered perfectly, with precise proportions of fats, carbohydrates, and proteins, down to the gram. Otherwise, it isn't safe and can be deadly. Every piece of food must be weighed, and only certain brands of food that correspond to ketogenic recipes can be used (alternative brands might have a different nutritional composition). Total calories must be closely monitored as well. The ketone bodies in the child's body must also be tracked daily to ensure that they aren't too high.

After two weeks of being on the ketogenic diet, Ella's seizures suddenly stopped. Then, two days later, on Easter Sunday, Ella smiled and laughed for the first time in six months. Lisa and Brian couldn't believe it. Within months, Ella came off many of her anticonvulsant medications, and she started becoming Ella again. She even began using words and talking. The ketogenic diet was working. As they watched Ella transform into a playful child before their very eyes, Lisa and Brian's dreams for Ella—now reimagined—slowly came back.

Ella started preschool and got back into her physical therapy sessions. She also started using a Gator, a gait-training wheelchair similar to an adult walker, with a sling for the child to sit on. In the fall of 2009, Lisa and Brian went to their first parent-teacher conference at Ella's school. As they walked into the classroom, Brian noticed Ella's Gator in the corner, but the sling was disconnected. He went over to the corner and reconnected the sling. When he mentioned this to Ella's teacher, she looked puzzled. "Ella doesn't use the sling, Brian," she said. "She just stands up and uses the Gator as a walker." Lisa and Brian were awestruck. "She's walking?" Brian exclaimed.

Ella had been using the sling on her Gator at home, but at school, her teachers had encouraged her to walk, not sit, while she was in the Gator. Lisa and Brian were excited that Ella was walking, but they were even more excited that she had been defying them, and that she knew what she could and couldn't get away with at home versus school.

In the spring of 2010, Ella's school held its annual concert. Lisa and Brian remember watching with wonder as Ella danced through the whole thing, even during the parts of the concert when she wasn't supposed to be dancing. She was like the child who memorizes not just her lines for the play, but all her friends' lines, too; she knew everyone's dance moves. Rather than asking Ella to stop dancing or sit down because it wasn't her turn, her teachers and classmates let her move to the music. The audience's eyes were glued on Ella.

Ella was back, and Lisa and Brian were also coming together more and more in the fight against their daughter's epilepsy. Ella had given them a new perspective about life. "You see the world totally differently," Brian said. "The little things start to have more meaning. We find wonder in the little things that Ella does. And she keeps our wonder-radars calibrated. There isn't an in-between for parents of a child with special needs. The child will either drive the parents apart or push them together."

For nearly a year and a half, the ketogenic diet and a moderate amount of anticonvulsant medication kept Ella's seizures at bay. She was also making progress during her therapy sessions. Her big goal was to walk unassisted, which seemed achievable, given the progress she was making. Whenever she was at school or around other children, Ella continued to be the life of the party.

But unfortunately, Ella's seizures started up again. Lisa and Brian had known that they would likely come back, but hadn't known when it would happen. This time around, at least at first, the seizures seemed less strong than before Ella had started the ketogenic diet. Even so, they began to slowly steal Ella's personality away from her again.

Ella's medical team made adjustments to her diet, varying the ratio of fats, carbohydrates, and proteins, and also altered her anticonvulsant regimen, experimenting with different medications, dosages, and administration schedules. Some of the combinations worked, reducing Ella's seizures for several weeks or even months, but the stability never lasted. The seizures always came back, and as time went on, they seemed to get worse and worse. Brian likened Ella's situation to an unstable dam: "Her seizures are the river. The ketogenic diet and her meds are the dam—and we have to keep rebuilding it."

Ella's seizures were now worse than they had been before the ketogenic diet. Every day was a struggle, and every day Lisa and Brian woke up wondering whether it would be Ella's last. Ella's medical team was out of ideas, so Lisa and Brian turned toward online epilepsy support groups and networks. As they read the message boards online, they found something unexpected: an underground army of parents was using marijuana extracts in oil form to treat their children's refractory epilepsy.

"I was reading about parents doing ghetto pharmacy in their backyards with marijuana," Lisa said. "But it was inspiring, and the results were promising."

Before they knew it, Lisa and Brian were talking to local marijuana growers, buying the plant, and setting up a makeshift lab in their kitchen. They packed long metal cooking cylinders with marijuana leaves, bought specialized coffee filters, blew highly flammable butane gas into the cylinders, and much more—all to extract a small amount of cannabis oil that could be mixed into Ella's food.

But there was a problem: Ella didn't seem to be responding to it. In fact, if anything, her seizures were worsening. At their wits' end, Lisa and Brian decided to travel to Colorado to consult with some of the experts who were on the front lines of using cannabis oils to treat seizures.

The trip turned out to be one of the best things they ever did. The first thing Lisa and Brian realized was that they felt safest buying cannabis oil from suppliers who knew the exact cannabidiol–tetrahydrocannabinol (CBD–THC) ratio of the oil they were producing. The second thing they learned was that Ella might do better with a more balanced CBD–THC ratio, rather than the high-CBD and low-THC oil they had been using.

Ever since then, under the guidance of the experts

they met in Colorado and Ella's medical team in Michigan, Lisa and Brian have been using various cannabis oil strains with varying CBD–THC ratios for their daughter. Ella has good days and bad days. But everyone on Ella's team is still working hard to find the best combination of therapies—medications, ketogenic diet, and cannabis oils—for Ella.

Meanwhile, Ella continues to be Ella. She loves Barbies, being silly, elbow-bumping, gymnastics, and cuddling. Lisa and Brian have the same amount of love for Ella that any parent would have for his or her child. That love gets them out of bed each day to face whatever Ella has in store for them.

But when it comes to inspiration, Lisa and Brian have a little bit of an edge. Because something as simple as Ella's getting into a car and shutting the door now brings them wonder. And wonder is one of the most inspiring forces we know.

●━━●

What does the playful quality of wonder look like, physiologically? On a neurophysiological level, wonder is an emotion. Nearly all emotions involve the limbic system in the brain, a group of subcortical structures that includes the hypothalamus, hippocampus, and amygdala. Wonder also involves the association cortex within the cerebral cortex. When a sensory stimulus provides new and expansive challenges to our existing limbic and associative circuitry, that's when we feel wonder. And while we are feeling wonder, the limbic system and the association cortex work together to process what is happening and assign significance to it. For example, for Lisa and Brian Dover, any progress that Ella makes, no matter the extent, sparks their limbic and associative neurons and, in turn, their senses of wonder. Simply put, when someone or something makes us pause in a meaningful way, we experience wonder as a warm, positive feeling that makes us feel as though time is standing still. In fact, one of the big benefits of wonder is its ability to keep us in the present moment. Wonder does this by stopping us and urging inaction rather than action. In this sense, it is different from most other emotions, which usually prompt us to act. This inaction reduces inflammation in our bodies, which helps stave off cardiovascular disease and cancer. It also allows us time to regroup and reflect, and also to become more inspired, trusting, and supportive.

Ella's story is very instructive in this way. Parents of a child with special needs must first learn to cope with the reality that their child is not who they thought he or she would be. But once they realize that it's not about canceling the dreams they had for their child, but rather reimagining them, they will often be able to experience very deep feelings of contentment. Wonder thresholds play a big part in this.

Ella keeps Lisa and Brian's thresholds for wonder low. She brings them back to the basics of life, well-being, and parenting, and basics are fertile ground for wonder. In his book *Far from the Tree*, which is about exceptional children and their families, Andrew Solomon alludes to this concept: "The disabled child becomes a glowing family hearth around which all gather in shared song."

There are many days in Ella's life, of course, when her seizures are unrelenting and hope is dim. But every small win of Ella's gently rouses Lisa and Brian's senses of wonder: when Ella's speech slowly improved with the cannabis oils; when she belly-laughed so hard that she couldn't stand up straight; when a little boy held the door for her and she was so thankful that she gave him a big kiss right on the lips; when she had everyone wrapped around her finger at the pediatric neurologist's office; when she heard a baby crying at the mall and needed to make sure that the baby wasn't hurting. Perhaps the biggest way that Ella has spoken to her parents' senses of wonder is through her small acts of defiance. All of these moments, most of them unexpected, have kindled Lisa and Brian's senses of wonder in amazing ways.

John Muir, famed leader of the American nature preservation movement, founding president of the Sierra Club, and mastermind behind the United States National Park System, experienced most of his wonder through nature. The important lesson that Muir imparted, however, through his journals and letters wasn't that we should simply commune with nature to experience wonder (although he did advocate this). Rather, it was to consciously maintain a perception that is open to wonder—in other words, have a *low* threshold for wonder. One of Muir's biographers, Michael Cohen, put this lesson well: "If a reader learned anything from [Muir's] narration, it was not what to see, but how to see it . . . . He tried to make his readers powerful and enthusiastic observers, like himself."

Muir's lesson was that the playful quality of wonder

is about *how* one is seeing and experiencing the world, not *what* one is seeing and experiencing. This means being open to discovering small moments of wonder in all things, big and small, and even those that at first may seem mundane and boring. It's easy to experience wonder when we are standing in front of a breathtaking nature scene or a beautiful masterpiece. But real mastery comes when we are able to experience wonder in the absence of the grand and majestic.

Similar to Muir, Walt Whitman observed the world through a wonder-tinted lens, too. His friend and biographer, Dr. Maurice Bucke, once said of Whitman:

> Strolling through a city or through a forest—it was evident that these things gave him a pleasure far beyond what they gave to ordinary people. Until I knew the man, it had not occurred to me that someone could derive so much absolute happiness from these things as he did. Perhaps no man who ever lived liked so many things and disliked so few as Walt Whitman. All natural objects seemed to have a charm for him. All sights and sounds seemed to please him.

Thinking about experiencing the world from a more wondrous predisposition means having a low threshold for wonder itself. This is analogous to the notion of having a low threshold for laughter, as discussed in Chapter 3. In other words, if one's threshold for wonder is too high, taking time to smell the roses is useless (because the smell will never produce an effect). Similarly, it's tough to feel a sense of wonder when it can only be produced by a new experience. A "been there, done that" attitude dulls the potential to feel wonder.

Despite all the great things that they do for us, moments of wonder are few and far between in adulthood. This, in large part, is because our wonder thresholds are too high. Conversely, children are often in a constant state of wonder because they are always experiencing something new, and their thresholds are low. To compensate for diminished novelty in adult life, wonder researchers suggest that adults slow down and open themselves up to new experiences. The idea is that slowness creates more opportunities for experiencing wonder. If you are moving through life too fast, nothing will ever catch your eye or be interesting enough to elicit wonder. And by being more open to new experiences, you will naturally increase novelty in your life and, in turn, your odds of experiencing wonder.

Although these two suggestions (slowing down and new experiences) are helpful, they don't guarantee a wonder-filled experience. Even when we do allow ourselves to slow down or experience something new, wonder will still be elusive if our wonder thresholds remain high.

This gets back to the lesson we can all learn from Ella Dover. If we can bring ourselves to be just a little more watchful of the wonder inside children, in all its simplicity and however it may appear, we'll be reminded of its importance and power in our own lives. We will also be more apt to keep our wonder thresholds at low and reachable levels.

As a child in the early 1900s, Rachel Carson kept to herself for the most part. She enjoyed exploring the woods near her home in Springdale, Pennsylvania. Playing alongside small creeks, Rachel marveled at the wildflowers and insects at the water's edge. Sometimes she would lie on her back and gaze through the treetops, watching clouds and birds pass by.

Rachel attended Pennsylvania College for Women (now Chatham College), where she majored in zoology. She then earned her master's degree in marine zoology at Johns Hopkins University. The Fish and Wildlife Service hired her shortly after she graduated. There, Rachel enjoyed a long tenure, first as an aquatic biologist and information specialist, and later as chief writer and editor for the agency's various publications.

Throughout the 1940s and '50s, Rachel wrote several books about marine life, ecology, and the environment. In the early 1960s, she wrote *Silent Spring*, which vaulted her into the national spotlight as a leading voice of the environmental movement. In *Silent Spring*, Rachel wrote about how the widespread use of the insecticide dichlorodiphenyltrichloroethane (DDT) was damaging wildlife, agricultural animals, pets, and even humans. The book stirred a public outcry that led to a governmental ban on agricultural use of DDT in the United States.

In her writings, Rachel strove to cultivate in her readers a deep reverence for life. This was what she had developed during her childhood musings in the woods, her days as an aquatic biologist, and her work for the governmental agency that protects all of nature's life-forms.

This reverence for life came full circle for Rachel

when she received word that her niece had died. Despite being in her late forties, Rachel took to raising her niece's son, Roger, who was an infant at the time of his mother's death. With no children of her own, Rachel thought carefully about how to best raise her grandnephew. It was important to her that Roger be exposed to nature. From the very start, Rachel took him on nature adventures and continued them throughout his childhood. Rachel would later write:

> It was hardly a conventional way to entertain one so young, I suppose. But now, with Roger a little past his fourth birthday, we are continuing that sharing of adventures in the world of nature that we began in his babyhood. And I think the results are good. The sharing includes nature in storm as well as calm, by night as well as day, and is based on having fun together rather than on teaching.

Rachel molded her and Roger's nature adventures into an article for *Woman's Home Companion*, titled "Help Your Child to Wonder." The article was later combined with photographs to form the book *A Sense of Wonder*, which was published after Rachel's death. In the book, Rachel beautifully describes many of the adventures she and Roger shared, such as this one with lichens:

> Having always loved the lichens because they have a quality of fairyland—silver rings on a stone, odd little forms like bones or horns or the shell of a sea creature—I was glad to find

Roger noticing and responding to the magic
change in their appearance wrought by the rain.
The woods path was carpeted with the so-called
reindeer moss. In dry weather, the lichen carpet
seems thin; it is brittle and crumbles underfoot.
Now, saturated with rain, which it absorbs like a
sponge, it was deep and springy. Roger delighted
in its texture, getting down on chubby knees to
feel it, and running from one patch to another, to
jump up and down in the deep, resilient carpet
with squeals of pleasure.

By this time in her life, Rachel, like Muir years before, had developed a tremendous sense of wonder from
her experiences with nature. She hoped that *A Sense of
Wonder* would encourage parents to expose their children
to nature early on, and that this nature-inspired sense of
wonder would travel with them into adulthood and beyond. As Rachel put it:

A child's world is fresh and new and beautiful,
full of wonder and excitement. It is our misfortune
that for most of us that clear-eyed vision, that true
instinct for what is beautiful and awe-inspiring, is
dimmed and even lost before we reach adulthood.
If I had influence with the good fairy who is supposed to preside over the christening of all children, I should ask that her gift to each child in the
world be a sense of wonder so indestructible that
it would last throughout life, as an unfailing antidote against the boredom and disenchantments of
later years, the sterile preoccupation with things

that are artificial, the alienation from the sources of our strength.

Rachel died from complications of breast cancer in 1964, when she was only fifty-six years old. She received multiple awards and honors for her lasting contributions to environmental awareness and policy, including the Audubon Medal, the Cullum Geographical Medal, and induction into the American Academy of Arts and Letters. She was also posthumously awarded the Presidential Medal of Freedom by Jimmy Carter.

Yet above all the well-deserved recognition, Rachel wanted her legacy to speak to the importance of keeping one's life open to and ready for wonder. For Rachel, this meant keeping a low threshold for wonder, but also engaging in experiences that had good odds of sparking wonder. These experiences can be almost anything—especially if one's wonder threshold is low—such as nature, the arts, human performance, and spirituality, to name a few. And, of course, noticing the wonder experienced by the children around us.

Interestingly, a closer look at the story of Rachel and Roger reveals that their nature adventures contained two distinct ways for Rachel to experience wonder: one that Rachel and Roger experienced together, and one that Rachel experienced alone. They both experienced wonder through nature. This was obvious. But Rachel also allowed herself to experience wonder *through* Roger. As she describes, each time Roger experienced wonder—whether it was watching waves thunder onto the shore, searching for ghost crabs on the beach, feeling the texture of wet lichens, or eyeing the misty river of the Milky Way—Rachel noticed wonder in Roger and felt it in herself, too. This is the important point. When it comes to lowering one's threshold for wonder, becoming more conscious of the wonder that children experience is sometimes the best place to start. For one thing, we are usually around children (even if we don't have children of our own) more often than wonder-inspiring stimuli. But more important, if we are experiencing wonder only through the grand and majestic, then our thresholds for wonder will keep rising. In other words, if it takes the Grand Canyon to feel a sense of wonder, the mind will eventually require more than the Grand Canyon.

When we stop and watch a child experience wonder, we notice not only the pureness of the emotion in the child's face, but also how low a child's threshold for wonder is. This helps remind us of the importance of savoring the small moments in life *and* having a low threshold for wonder ourselves. Grandparents and older adults know this wisdom well. Older adults, especially retirees, generally don't have the same degree of adult responsibilities that they once had. They have also survived their crazy-busy middle years and know what is and isn't important in life. All of this culminates in a remarkable capacity for watching and reveling in the moments of wonder that grandchildren or other children in their lives experience.

I know this all may sound a little far-fetched. We all know—especially those of us who are parents—that children can sometimes be very challenging and hard to be around. We also know that wonder is often the last thing that comes to mind when kids are being difficult, such as when we've already said "no" twice to the pack of gum in the grocery store checkout lane. But being ready for moments of wonder in children, even when they are being unruly, can help us do the right thing when the going gets rough. Remember, wonder slows us down and makes us more supportive, both of which a child desperately needs—our patience and support—when big feelings are in the air.

In the playfully intelligent people I have studied, the majority of them err on the side of wonder rather than annoyance in their interactions with children. Sure, they get annoyed with their kids every now and then. But, in general, they truly enjoy watching how children encounter the world. This wonder-ready approach toward children helps them maintain a low threshold for wonder in their lives.

Glennon Doyle, founder of the popular parenting blog *Momastery* and best-selling author of *Carry On, Warrior*, expressed this concept in a slightly different way in an article she wrote in 2012 for the *Huffington Post*. In the article, titled "Don't Carpe Diem," she talks about how she, as a parent of young children, is constantly being bombarded by seize-the-day messaging. As an example, Glennon explains that people, usually charming older ladies, approach her in the grocery store or Target checkout lane when her kids are going bonkers and say things like, "Enjoy every moment. This time goes by so fast." Glennon always replies with something respectful, such as: "Thank you. Yes, the time goes fast. Thanks." But in reality, she's thinking, "Are you freaking kidding me? Parenting is damn hard! I can't wait for these kids to go to bed!"

Her point in the article is that she used to worry about

not doing a good job as a parent *and* not seizing every moment of her parenting journey as pure joy. Worries that every parent has felt. But now, rather than a carpe diem philosophy, Glennon looks out for something that she calls "kairos time." Here's how she described it:

> There are two different types of time. Chronos time is what we live in. It's regular time. It's one minute at a time. It's staring down the clock till bedtime time. It's ten excruciating minutes in the Target line time. It's four screaming minutes in time-out time. It's two hours till daddy gets home time. Chronos is the hard, slow-passing time we parents often live in.
>
> Then there's kairos time. Kairos is God's time. It's time outside of time. It's metaphysical time. It's those magical moments in which time stands still. I have a few of those moments each day. And I cherish them.
>
> Like when I actually stop what I'm doing and really look at Tish. I notice how perfectly smooth and brownish her skin is. I notice the perfect curves of her teeny elf mouth and her Asian-ish brown eyes, and I breathe in her soft Tishy smell. In these moments, I see that her mouth is moving, but I can't hear her because all I can think is, "This is the first time I've really *seen* Tish all day, and my God, she is so beautiful." Kairos.

Glennon goes on to describe how, even though kairos moments are fleeting, she marks them in her mind whenever they happen. At the end of each day, she may not remember exactly what they were or how many she experienced, but she does remember that she had them.

Glennon's kairos time is the experience of wonder in the daily struggle of adult life. And her message is that it's possible. It's possible to experience wonder in adulthood, apart from the grand and majestic, in a way that beautifully reconnects us to our childhoods and allows us to see the world as if through a child's eyes. This is the magic of the playful quality of wonder. Wonder, more so than the other four playful qualities that have been discussed in this book, urges us to say hello again to the child inside of us and face adulthood with a lighter perspective that is ripe with contentment, meaning, and joy—one that helps us awaken every day with a fearless enthusiasm.

This brings us to one final note that involves Emily Perl Kingsley, one of the longest tenured writers for the beloved children's television show *Sesame Street*. Emily started writing for the show in 1970, and she has received seventeen Emmy Awards and fourteen more Emmy nominations for her work.

One of Emily's biggest contributions to the show was her groundbreaking work on including individuals with disabilities. She has received numerous accolades for this. Part of her motivation to venture into the uncharted territory of disability in television was her own personal experience with her son, Jason, who was born with Down syndrome in 1974.

In 1987, reflecting on her experience raising Jason, Emily wrote a short, modern fable about what it's like to raise a child with a disability, called "Welcome to Holland":

I am often asked to describe the experience of raising a child with a disability—to try to help people who have not shared that unique experience to understand it, to imagine how it would feel. It's like this . . .

When you're going to have a baby, it's like planning a fabulous vacation trip—to Italy. You buy a bunch of guidebooks and make your wonderful plans. The Colosseum. The Michelangelo *David*. The gondolas in Venice. You may learn some handy phrases in Italian. It's all very exciting.

After months of eager anticipation, the day finally arrives. You pack your bags and off you go. Several hours later, the plane lands. The stewardess comes in and says, "Welcome to Holland."

"Holland?!?!" you say. "What do you mean Holland? I signed up for Italy! I'm supposed to be in Italy. All my life I've dreamed of going to Italy."

But there's been a change in flight plan. They've landed in Holland and there you must stay.

The important thing is they haven't taken you to a horrible, disgusting, filthy place full of pestilence, famine, and disease. It's just a different place.

So you must go out and buy new guidebooks. And you must learn a whole new language. And you will meet a whole new group of people you would never have met.

It's just a different place. It's slower paced than Italy, less flashy than Italy. But after you've been there for a while and you catch your breath, you look around . . . and you begin to notice that Holland has windmills . . . and Holland has tulips. Holland even has Rembrandts.

But everyone you know is busy coming and going from Italy . . . and they're all bragging about what a wonderful time they had there. And for the rest of your life, you will say, "Yes, that's where I was supposed to go. That's what I had planned."

And the pain of that will never, ever, ever, ever go away . . . because the loss of that dream is a very, very significant loss.

But . . . if you spend the rest of your life mourning the fact that you didn't get to Italy, you may never be free to enjoy the very special, the very lovely things . . . about Holland.

Wonder isn't about *what* we are seeing and experiencing. It's about *how* we are seeing and processing our experiences.

Holland is all around us.

Wonder Well Played

Wonder Rehab

For most of us, by the time we reach adulthood, our thresholds for wonder have gone from being very low as children to very high as adults. Often, only the spectacular can bring us to a state of wonder. This can be exhausting and disheartening, leave us short on wonder, and keep us from enjoying all the great benefits that wonder affords.

This is why wonder rehab is so important. Like a physical injury that requires conscious, deliberate, and committed rehabilitation to ensure proper healing, our high thresholds for wonder in adulthood can also benefit from a rehabilitation program.

The program is simple. It's three suggestions that can be repeated as often as necessary. The goals of the program are to lower one's threshold for experiencing wonder in the near term and then help keep it low for years to come. Here are the three suggestions:

1. **Find the mini-moment.** It's certainly worthwhile to make time for and seek out grand and majestic experiences, whether they're natural, artistic, musical, spiritual, or the like. But remember, if it always takes the spectacular to stir your sense of wonder, this can work against you in the long run. One thing that can help is to find one mini-moment of wonder that is hidden

somewhere amid the grand and majestic. Maybe it will come from paying close attention to how wonder is unfolding inside someone standing or sitting near you. Maybe it will be an unexpectedly kind gesture that you observe or a positive interaction that you see occurring between two people. Whatever it looks like, being on the lookout for mini-moments of wonder within the spectacular will remind you of the importance of finding wonder in regular adult life and also help keep your threshold low and reachable.

2. **Remember the mini-you.** Periodically, take a moment to recall a positive memory from your childhood. It doesn't have to be extravagant. In fact, simple memories tend to work best. Perhaps it's the joy you felt when you played a favorite game with a childhood pal. Or maybe it's a warm feeling you had when you and your family enjoyed a tradition together. This exercise will help keep you connected to your childhood and also remind you of what it feels like to have a low threshold for wonder. The one catch is that it's much easier to remember our bad childhood memories than our good ones. Negative feelings involve more neural processing than positive feelings and thus are remembered better. So don't be too hard on yourself if you have to keep using the same positive memories over and over. That's perfectly normal and can still be effective.

3. **Observe the minis around you.** Whether you have children or not, try to become a keen observer of the wonder that emanates from the children you come in contact with. If a metal detector can find buried trea-

sures in the sand on a beach, your goal is to nurture a wonder detector that finds and appreciates the wonder in children—something that is often buried and out of sight of the adult eye.

The Rainbow Hallway

My third year of medical school at the University of Virginia was coming to a close, and I was in the final week of my family medicine clerkship. For the clerkship, students spent some time shadowing family physicians at various clinics across the state of Virginia. This gave students an opportunity to learn about medicine that happens outside the walls of hospitals.

I was shipped to Pearisburg, Virginia, a small town nestled in the Appalachian Mountains. My mentor had been practicing there for more than twenty years. He had buzzed salt-and-pepper hair and a contagious smile. Everyone in Pearisburg knew and loved him. He was smart, but equally humble, and incredibly kind.

Whether it was offering reassurance or simply being present during a difficult moment, he was nothing short of Picasso when it came to the art of medicine. *Not* doing was his greatest strength, and his patients respected him for it. "Anthony," he said on my first day, "in the course of your training, you will learn every detail of what we *do* for patients, from prescribing medicine to procedures and surgeries. Never forget the power of just being there with them."

On the Thursday afternoon of my final week, my mentor and I had just finished with his last patient of the day. We were packing up our bags and completing his notes when he said, "Anthony, don't worry about coming in tomorrow."

"What do you mean?" I asked.

"Well, instead, I need a favor."

"Sure, anything," I replied.

"I want you to see a patient of mine, Mrs. Eleanor Schaeffer."

"Is she in the hospital?"

"No, she's at her home. She lives alone, on the outskirts of town."

"You want me to see her at her home?" I asked.

"Yes, I want you to do a house call."

"Oh, okay, sounds great. Is there anything I should know about her beforehand?"

"Yes, Eleanor has terminal lung cancer. She won't be with us much longer, and she wants to be home as much as possible. She's also a bit eccentric, in a good way. You'll see what I mean when you meet her."

I had never done a house call before. In fact, I didn't realize they still existed. Feeling both eager and nervous, I gave my mentor a hug and thanked him for a great clerkship.

The next morning, I hit the road early. I arrived at Mrs. Schaeffer's house and parked my car on the street. Her stately, Queen Anne-style home was situated on a tall hill. A long, red-brick walkway led to her front door. With white-painted wood siding and black shutters, the exterior of the home was well preserved. I exited my car and started walking toward her house. When I was about ten feet up the walkway, I noticed something on the front door. It was a letter-sized sheet of yellow paper. I thought that it might be a note from Mrs. Schaeffer. Perhaps she'd had to run an errand or had gone out for a walk. I picked up my pace. As I approached the door, I saw more clearly what the yellow piece of paper was. There were several lines of small text in the middle of it. Mrs. Schaeffer's signature appeared toward the bottom, and across the top—in large black letters—read:

DO NOT RESUSCITATE

Mrs. Schaeffer had taped a Do Not Resuscitate (DNR) order to her front door. Terminal patients who are spending their remaining days in their homes and do not want heroic measures used to save their lives sometimes post such DNR orders. This way, their wishes are made known to emergency personnel who might be called to their homes.

I knocked. Mrs. Schaeffer opened the door and greeted me with a smile. "I've been expecting you, Anthony. Come right in, and please call me Eleanor."

Eleanor was in her seventies. She was wearing a flower-patterned dress. Her thin, white hair was shoulder-length, and it glistened in the sunlight. I stepped through the doorway and started taking off my shoes, but Eleanor grabbed my hand and ushered me into her living room. "Don't worry about your shoes," she said. She sat

down on a Victorian parlor chair and motioned for me to
find a seat on her red sofa. Our conversation began.

"Welcome, Anthony. I'm glad you're here."

"Me, too, Mrs. Schaeffer . . . I mean Eleanor. I won't
take up too much of your time. I'm a third-year medical
student at the University of Virginia, and your prima-
ry-care physician asked me to—"

"You take all the time you need," Eleanor interrupt-
ed. "I don't have anywhere else I need to be!"

"Thanks," I said. "I've never done a house call before."

"There's a first time for everything, Anthony."

"Right," I replied. "Let's get started with how you
have been feeling. How have you been feeling? Is your
breathing labored? Are you in pain?"

"Too many questions at once, Anthony. Ask your
patients one question at a time. Wait for their response.
Then ask your next question. It's like breathing. Exhale
before you inhale again."

"I'm sorry, ma'am. I'm a little nervous."

"Ma'am?"

"Uh . . . I mean Eleanor."

"No more mistakes on the name. Throw your nervousness out the window, Anthony." Eleanor smiled and flung
her hand up toward the window that was behind her chair.

"I'm feeling pretty good today," she continued. "Some
days are better than others. My breathing is about the
same. Oxygen at night drives me nuts—that cannula in
my nose. No pain, thank goodness."

"How's your energy level?" I asked.

"I've lived most of my life with a lot of energy. The

cancer has probably reduced me to a normal level." Eleanor chuckled.

We continued to talk about her symptoms and medications for a few more minutes. I took her blood pressure with a portable cuff that I had brought with me. I also listened to her lungs with my stethoscope, but as I finished her upper-lung fields and was moving toward her lower ones, Eleanor backed away from me.

"Let's put that away, Anthony," Eleanor said, taking the stethoscope from my ears and tucking it into my white coat. "I know what you are supposed to do and that you're learning, but today, I want you to think outside your textbook. Look at me as a human being who is sitting next to you—a human being who happens to be dying, but a human being nonetheless. Let's have a few laughs and share a few stories about our lives. Stories connect us to one another and are sometimes all we have in the end."

Somewhat taken aback, I sat down again on the red sofa. I understood what Eleanor was saying, but I hadn't expected the house call to go in this direction. Over the next hour or so, she served us lemonade and pastries, and we openly shared stories from our lives. Some were serious and some were light. I told her that my mom had recently been diagnosed with cancer and that meeting my wife, Anna, was the best thing that had ever happened to me. We laughed over funny moments from our respective weddings. Eleanor talked about her late husband and their love story. We giggled about little personal quirks— such as how she loved offering people mints the instant she detected bad breath, and how I always ate a bowl of cereal before going to bed.

At one point, Eleanor went over to a cabinet in the corner of her living room and brought out a large three-ring binder. I thought it was a photo album, but it was a collection of poems that she had saved over the years. She called it her "Book of Funny Poems." All the poems were humorous to her.

"A poem had to make me laugh, but also think, to get into this book," she said.

We read some of the poems out loud, at times bowling over with laughter. Afterward, I mentioned that I should be getting on my way. Eleanor asked me to follow her to the kitchen. So we walked through the living room to the kitchen, which was in the back of her house. We put our dishes in the sink. Then Eleanor motioned me down the hallway that connected her kitchen to her front door.

I started walking down the hallway, which I had not seen when I first walked into her home because Eleanor had taken me straight to her living room before I could take my shoes off. She hadn't wanted me to see the hallway at first, but now she did.

As I walked down it, I began to feel as though our entire visit had been leading up to her hallway. I was speechless. Eleanor was silent, too, but I could hear her footsteps right behind me. She knew there would be silence as I stared at the hallway's walls and ceiling. Letter-sized sheets of red, orange, yellow, green, blue, and purple paper covered every square inch. And on every sheet—in bold black letters—read:

DO NOT RESUSCITATE

The sheets of paper were colorful photocopies of the DNR order taped to the outside of her front door. It felt as though I were walking underneath a rainbow.

When we finally reached the front of her house, I looked back; Eleanor was right behind me, grinning.

"Are you okay?" she asked.

"I think so," I said.

"Good."

"Thanks for having me."

"You're welcome. Now, move along. You need to go and give that Anna of yours a big hug."

I stepped out the front door and started walking down the red-brick walkway to my car. When I had gone about halfway, I looked back. Eleanor was standing in the doorway.

"One more thing," I called back to her. "Why the rainbow hallway of DNR orders?"

"Oh, Anthony," she laughed. "You see—I just don't want anyone to make a mistake and bring me back to life! I also want people to have a moment in their days that freezes in time. We are always in such a hurry, you know. Besides, this hallway is one more thing for my family and friends to laugh about at my funeral."

We both laughed and then exchanged silent nods. I got into my car, waved, and drove away.

That day would be the first and last time that I would see Eleanor. Several weeks later, she passed away comfortably—in her home.

•━━━•

It has taken me nearly ten years to realize and fully understand the wisdom that Eleanor offered me that day. I
sometimes wonder whether she could sense how the intensity of adulthood was starting to take hold of my life.
Maybe she just knew that it always, at some level, takes
hold of all of our lives. Perhaps she was betting that my
life would become increasingly busy and hectic. Maybe
she was also hoping that when it did, I would remember
the stories and laughter that we shared together—and
then see her motioning me down the hallway.

"One more thing to laugh about . . . at my funeral."

Eleanor's lesson was that nurturing our inner playground throughout our lives is, in the end, very much worth
our time. Most of us, in the end, want some laughter (as
well as some tears) at our funerals. We want to be missed,
but we also want to be remembered for our good character
and for seeing and appreciating the lighter side of life, not
to mention the lighter, imperfect parts of our own selves.

American political and cultural commentator David Brooks has spoken about what he calls "résumé virtues" and "eulogy virtues." Résumé virtues, as Brooks
described them, are what one brings to the marketplace
of society. They are your skill set, the work you do, and
the contributions you have made and are making for the
greater good. But eulogy virtues are what your family and
friends talk about at your funeral: the kind of person you
were, your character, and how deeply you loved and were
loved.

Both categories of virtues are important in different
ways. But as Brooks noted, "our culture and our educa-
tional systems spend more time teaching the skills and

strategies you need for career success (résumé) than the qualities you need to radiate that sort of inner light (eulogy)."

Qualities like imagination, which helps us reframe and empathize; sociability, which resists first impressions but relies on humility to take our relationships to new heights; humor, which strengthens our connections with others and keeps us moving through our deserts; spontaneity, which lubricates our mental flexibilities and invigorates our generosities; and wonder, which keeps life's amusement park within arm's reach.

Our inner light radiates most brightly when we understand how playfulness can change our lives, beyond the surface. Having this knowledge, this intelligence, preserves the playful part of our personalities—our internal Joylands—amid the stress and seriousness of adulthood. It becomes the Jiminy Cricket inside our minds, reminding us that playfulness has tremendous value in the here and now.

And the icing on the cake? A specific type of neuron in our brains, called a mirror neuron, is responsible for the monkey-see, monkey-do phenomenon. Mirror neurons explain our ability to understand another person's actions and behaviors, and allow us to effectively imitate what we deem valuable. When we do imitate beneficial behaviors, our brains rewire to make the behaviors a more permanent part of us. So, as we consciously consider and use playful qualities in our lives, others will witness the benefits, and do the same. That's the ripple effect of living a playfully intelligent life. And it's good news for us old dogs, too—we can learn new tricks.

So crack a smile, stand up, and take a deep breath or two. Your playful intelligence is ready to pick up where it left off many years ago, joining you again on this trek of life that we are all trying to make sense of and enjoy. It may work a little differently now, compared to then.

But that's the exciting part—because so do you.

Acknowledgments

This book required more of me than I initially thought it would when the idea for it first entered my mind nearly five years ago. My wife, Anna, and our daughters have borne the greatest burden in this regard, since I spent many nights, weekends, and Wednesday afternoons with my computer, rather than with them. Anna, Ava, Mia, and Lola: Thank you for your insights, unyielding patience, fierce support, and indestructible love every step of the way. You girls are my world, and I love you beyond measure.

I am indebted to Ryan Zaklin, who has been the ultimate right-hand man and consummate friend throughout this journey. Ryan helped me define and refine my vision and believed in the value of playful intelligence from the start. He also helped develop content for some of the case studies. Thank you, brother.

Besides Ryan, there are four people—Amy Nielander, Lisa Tener, Christy Fletcher, and Lisa Grubka—who, in unique ways, gave me their support for the project very early on. To the four of you, thank you for your original morsels of confidence.

This book never happens without the willingness of others to share their stories and work. Salvatore Maddi, Sheila R., Kellie Sprague, Anette Prehn, John Zeglis, Percy Strickland, Vivienne D., Dan D., Brenda Elsagher, Bob Sutherland, Don Gregory, David Rand, Christian

Smith, Lisa Dover, Brian Dover, Ella Dover, Ashley Jennings, Renee Shellhaas, and all my patients who allowed me the privilege of exploring the playful part of their personalities—my sincere gratitude for your contributions. I owe others as well. As I wrote, Karen Magnuson read the first draft of each chapter and provided real-time content and copy edits. Four readers—Lawrence Cohen, Melissa Talhelm, Erin Rosenberg, and Michael Rosenberg—reviewed the entire manuscript and made valuable comments on page after page. Jim Richardson helped sharpen the introduction. To all of you, thank you for bettering this book.

My extended family and friends graciously listened to concepts and ideas—often ad nauseam—that swam around my mind while I was researching and writing. They offered valuable feedback sometimes without even knowing it. Karen DeBenedet, Nelson DeBenedet, Millie Brooks, Rowan Brooks, Marjorie Kimble, Joe Kimble (who helped polish the Think Small story), MaryAnn Pierce, Lowell Timm, Kathi Timm, Nathan Timm, Kim Daly, Aaron Timm, Sandie Timm, Marc Larochelle, David Fuelling, Lenée Fuelling, Michael McNamara, Meredith McNamara, Cory Wernimont, Meghan Wernimont, Dyke McEwen, Laura McEwen, Mark Zeglis, Dan Neubauer, Randy Schrecengost, Kate McGeary, Kristin Burgard, Paul Burgard, Kari Nehro, Denny Nehro, Sandie Wankel, Darcy Stoll, Magic Bill Lockwood, Kathleen Mobley, Derek Mobley, Mary-Catherine Harrison, John Sarnecki, Gregg Hammerman, Sandro Tuccinardi, Monique Sluymers, Jason Slocum, Kate Slocum, Heather Shumaker, Tony Tsai, Joe Elmunzer, and my Huron Gastro,

Center for Digestive Care, Imaging Center, and Livingston families—thank you all.

Finally, I am forever grateful to my publisher, Jeffrey Goldman, my editor, Kate Murray, and the entire Santa Monica Press team for believing in this book and bringing it to life.

Notes

INTRODUCTION: *Restore Joyland*

- Information about Jiminy Cricket was gathered from the *New York Times* movie review of *Pinocchio* that was written by Frank Nugent in 1940: http://www.nytimes.com/movie/review?res=9A03E2D8113EE33ABC4053DFB466838B659EDE (accessed April 19, 2016).

- Howard Gardner's work and his multiple intelligences theory can be explored at www.howardgardner.com (accessed April 20, 2016).

- When investigating what defines adult playfulness, I relied most on the research of Careen Yarnal and Xinyi Qian, "Older-Adult Playfulness: An Innovative Construct and Measurement for Healthy Aging Research," American Journal of Play 4, no. 1 (2011): 52–79.

- The story of Joyland was developed through personal correspondence with Marlene Irvin in May 2016; http://cjonline.com/news/2015-10-25/wichita-woman-works-restore-joyland-carousel-horses (accessed May 10, 2016); http://www.kansas.com/news/article1094886.html (accessed May 10, 2016); http://www.kansas.com/news/article1146103.html (accessed May 12, 2016); and http://www.bizjournals.com/wichita/print-edition/2012/02/03/high-school-students-dream-plan-to.html (accessed May 13, 2016).

CHAPTER ONE: *Imagination*

- The Sal Maddi and Illinois Bell material was derived from Salvatore Maddi, *The Hardy Executive: Health Under Stress* (Homewood, IL: Dow Jones-Irwin, 1984), 1–32; Salvatore Maddi and Deborah Khoshaba, *Resilience at Work: How to Succeed No Matter What Life Throws at You* (New York: AMACOM, 2005), 15–39; information available at www.HardinessInstitute.com

(accessed September 20, 2014); and an interview with Sal on
October 29, 2014.

- Sheila R.'s story was developed from a clinical encounter on
September 21, 2013, an interview with Sheila on October 19,
2014, an interview with Sheila's oncologist, Dr. Kellie Sprague, on
October 29, 2014, an interview with Sheila's daughter Dyann on
October 30, 2014, an interview with Sheila's daughter Brenda on
October 30, 2014, and e-mail correspondence with Sheila in late
2014 and early 2015.

- Alex Osborn's material is from his landmark book *Applied
Imagination* (New York: Scribner, 1953), 69–85, 124.

- Anette Prehn's material was adapted from her article "Create
Reframing Mindsets through Framestorm," *NeuroLeadership
Journal* 4 (2012) as well as email correspondence with Anette in
August 2015. More information about Anette's work can be found
on her website: www.brainsmart.today.

- The material on the Einstellung Effect was adapted from Abraham
Luchins and Edith Hirsch, *Rigidity of Behavior: A Variational
Approach to the Effect of Einstellung* (Eugene, OR: University of
Oregon Books, 1959).

- The JFK-Khrushchev story was developed through the following
sources:
  - http://www.netplaces.com/john-f-kennedy/jfks-early-life/
    seeking-motherly-affection.htm (accessed November 2014).
  - Michael O'Brien, *John F. Kennedy: A Biography* (New York:
    Macmillan, 2005), 71.
  - Theodore S. Sorenson, *Kennedy* (New York: Konecky &
    Konecky, 1965), 282, 555.
  - Michael R. Beschloss, *The Crisis Years: Kennedy and
    Khrushchev* (New York: Edward Burlingame Books, 1991), 13.
  - FRUS Online: Letter from President Kennedy to Chairman
    Khrushchev, 22 February 1961, in *Foreign Relations of the
    United States, 1961–1963, Vol. 6, Washington* (Washington,
    DC: Department of State, 1996).
  - Philip A. Goduti, *Kennedy's Kitchen Cabinet and the Pursuit*

*of Peace: The Shaping of American Foreign Policy 1961–
1963* (Jefferson, NC: McFarland & Company, Incorporated
Publishers, 2009), 49.
- Srobe Talbott et al., *Khrushchev Remembers: The Glasnost Tapes*
(Boston: Little Brown and Company, 1990), 449.
- http://americacomesalive.com/2013/07/07/the-pets-of-
president-john-f-kennedys-family/#.VGC3staFzH0 (accessed
November 2014).
- http://history.state.gov/historicaldocuments/frus1961-63v06/
d17 (accessed November 2014).
- http://www.cubanmissilecrisis.org (accessed November 2014).
- J. G. Blight and J. M. Lang, *Fog of War: Lessons from the
Life of Robert S. McNamara* (Oxford: Rowman and Littlefield
Publishers, 2005), 34.
- Robert S. McNamara and James G. Blight, *Wilson's Ghost:
Reducing the Risk of Conflict, Killing, and Catastrophe in the
21st Century* (New York: Public Affairs, 2001), 72.
- http://www.hpu.edu/CHSS/History/GraduateDegree/
MADMSTheses/files/gintarejanulaityte.pdf (accessed
November 2014).
- Arthur M. Schleslinger, *A Thousand Days: John F. Kennedy in
the White House* (Boston: Riverside Press, 1965), 102.
• The material on the Susan J. Frank experiments was adapted from
her chapter entitled "Just Imagine How I Feel: How to Improve
Empathy through Training in Imagination," in *The Power of
Human Imagination: New Methods in Psychotherapy*, ed. Jerome
Singer and Kenneth Pope (New York: Springer, 1978), 309–46.
• The material on reading fiction and empathy was adapted from
Raymond Mar et al. "Bookworms versus Nerds: Exposure to
Fiction versus Non-Fiction, Divergent Associations with Social
Ability, and the Simulation of Fictional Social Worlds," *Journal of
Research in Personality* 40 (2006): 694–712.
• The Josie-Megan anecdote is based on a clinical encounter that
occurred in the summer of 2006 at a major academic hospital in
the United States. Some of the story's details have been changed to

protect the identities of the parties involved.

- Parts of the Reframe Readiness subsection were adapted from http://stress.about.com/od/positiveattitude/a/reframing.html (accessed December 3, 2014).

- Some of the material in the Empathize with Your Enemy subsection was adapted from Ralph K. White, *Fearful Warriors: A Psychological Profile of U.S.–Soviet Relations* (New York: Free Press, 1984).

- Material within the What a Day for a Daydream subsection was adapted from Matthew Killingsworth and Daniel Gilbert, "A Wandering Mind Is an Unhappy Mind," *Science* 330 (2010): 932; Raymond Mar et al., "How Daydreaming Relates to Life Satisfaction, Loneliness, and Social Support: The Importance of Gender and Daydream Content," *An International Journal* 21 (2011): 401–7; Jerome Singer, "Navigating the Stream of Consciousness: Research in Daydreaming and Related Inner Experience," *American Psychologist* 30 (1974): 727–38; and Peter F. Delaney et al., "Remembering to Forget: The Amnesic Effect of Daydreaming," *Psychological Science* 21 (2010): 1036–42.

CHAPTER TWO: *Sociability*

- Church Hill's decline and rise is discussed in John Murden, "High on the Hill," http://www.styleweekly.com/richmond/high-on-the-hill/Content?oid=1957386 (accessed January 31, 2015).

- John Johnson's quote about Church Hill's decline is noted in Rachel Kaufman, "History and Mystery in Richmond's Church Hill," http://www.washingtonpost.com/wp-dyn/content/article/2008/12/11/AR2008121103085.html (accessed January 31, 2015).

- Mary Wingfield Scott's association between Church Hill and slums is noted in her book *Old Richmond Neighborhoods* (Richmond, VA: Whittet & Shepperson, 1950), 53.

- Percy Strickland's and Church Hill Academy and Tutoring's story is gathered from personal correspondence with Percy Strickland (January and February 2015).

- The parable of the Good Samaritan is from the New International Version of the Bible, Luke 10: 25–37.
- Church Hill's crime statistics were compiled from the Richmond Police Department's Crime Incident Information Center at http://eservices.ci.richmond.va.us/applications/crimeinfo/index.asp (accessed February 7, 2015).
- According to *USA Today*, Church Hill is listed as an up-and-coming neighborhood at http://experience.usatoday.com/america/story/best-of-lists/2014/05/07/10-up-and-coming-neighborhoods-explore-this-summer/8814935/ (accessed February 7, 2015).
- The concept of anchoring bias is described in Amos Tversky and Daniel Kahneman, "Judgment under Uncertainty: Heuristics and Biases," *Science* 185, no. 4157 (1974): 1124–31.
- Is it California dreaming or true happiness? This is discussed in David Schkade and Daniel Kahneman, "Does Living in California Make People Happy? A Focusing Illusion in Judgments of Life Satisfaction," *Psychological Science* 9, no. 5 (1998): 340–46.
- The masterpiece on how we think with System 1 and System 2 is Daniel Kahenman's *Thinking, Fast and Slow* (New York: Farrar, Straus, and Giroux, 2013).
- The material on stereotypes (i.e., categorical person perception) is gathered from C. Neil Macrae and Galen V. Bodenhausen, "Social Cognition: Categorical Person Perception," *British Journal of Psychology* 92, no. 1 (2001): 239–55.
- The concept that there is great power in powerless communication is from Adam Grant's book *Give and Take: A Revolutionary Approach to Success* (New York: Viking, 2013), 126–54.
- The definition of "humility" was from http://www.merriam-webster.com/dictionary/humility (accessed February 8, 2015).
- The story of John Zeglis's humility was developed through personal correspondence with John in February and March 2015; http://business.illinois.edu/insight/summer99/ (accessed February 9, 2015); http://w4.stern.nyu.edu/accounting/docs/syllabi/Cases/AT&T%20Case.pdf (accessed March 10, 2015); and http://usatoday30.usatoday.com/money/industries/

telecom/2004-11-09-zeglis_x.htm (accessed February 8, 2015).

- Jim Collins's leadership research is discussed in "Level 5 Leadership: The Triumph of Humility and Fierce Resolve," http://hbr.org/2005/07/level-5-leadership-the-triumph-of-humility-and-fierce-resolve (accessed January 28, 2015).

- Seymour Sarason's story is adapted from his autobiography, *The Making of an American Psychologist* (San Francisco: Jossey-Bass, 1988), 13–23, 26–28, 145–57, and http://articles.courant.com/2010-02-28/features/hc-exlife0228.artfeb28_1_doctorate-in-clinical-psychology-seymour-b-sarason-pioneer (accessed February 8, 2015).

- Sense of community theory was derived from David W. McMillan and David M. Chavis, "Sense of Community: A Definition and Theory," *Journal of Community Psychology* 14 (1986): 6–23.

- The family that grazes together stays together. The material on family meals is adapted from http://www.gallup.com/poll/166628/families-routinely-dine-together-home.aspx (accessed March 7, 2015); Rachel Tumin and Sarah E. Anderson, "The Epidemiology of Family Meals among Ohio's Adults," *Public Health Nutrition* (September 2014): 1–8; and http://thefamilydinnerproject.org/ (accessed March 7, 2015).

- Ask your neighbor for ketchup more often, and then check out these great resources that helped build the material on the benefits of neighborhood togetherness: Brenda Egolf et al., "The Roseto Effect: A 50-Year Comparison of Mortality Rates," *American Journal of Public Health* 82 (1992): 1089–92; Malcolm Gladwell, *Outliers: The Story of Success* (New York: Little, Brown and Company, 2008), 3–11; and Ana V. Diez Roux and Christina Mair, "Neighborhoods and Health," *Annals of the New York Academy of Sciences* 1186 (2010): 125–45.

- Oxytocin information was gathered from Susan Pinker, *The Village Effect: How Face-to-Face Contact Can Make Us Healthier and Happier* (New York: Spiegel & Grau, 2014), 262–64; and http://www.apa.org/monitor/feb08/oxytocin.aspx (accessed March 18, 2015).

- The virtual-community material is adapted from Dar Meshi et al., "Nucleus Accumbens Response to Gains in Reputation for the Self Relative to Gains for Others Predicts Social Media Use," *Frontiers in Human Neuroscience* 7 (2013): 439; Hayeon Song et al., "Does Facebook Make You Lonely? A Meta-Analysis," *Computers in Human Behavior* 36 (2014): 446; Ethan Kross et al., "Facebook Use Predicts Declines in Subjective Well-Being in Young Adults," *PLOS ONE* 8 (2013): 8; Rosalind Barnett et al., "At-Risk Youth in After-School Programs: How Does Their Use of Media for Learning about Community Issues Relate to Their Perceptions of Community Connectedness, Community Involvement, and Community Support?," *Journal of Youth Development* 9 (2014): 157–69; Rebecca Schnall et al., "eHealth Interventions for HIV Prevention in High-Risk Men Who Have Sex with Men: A Systematic Review," *Journal of Medical Internet Research* 16 (2014): e134; Sean D. Young et al., "Social Networking Technologies as an Emerging Tool for HIV Prevention: A Cluster Randomized Trial," *Annals of Internal Medicine* 159, no. 5 (2013): 318–24; Renée K. Biss et al., "Distraction Can Reduce Age-Related Forgetting," *Psychological Science* 24, no. 4 (2013): 448–55; http://uanews.org/story/should-grandma-join-facebook-it-may-give-her-a-cognitive-boost-study-finds (accessed February 11, 2015); and http://www.exeter.ac.uk/news/research/title_426286_en.html (accessed February 11, 2015).
- The social isolation and loneliness material was adapted from John Cacioppo and William Patrick, *Loneliness: Human Nature and the Need for Social Connection* (New York: WW Norton and Company, 2008), 101–09, 162–63; Naomi I. Eisenberger et al., "Does Rejection Hurt? An fMRI Study of Social Exclusion," *Science* 302 (2003): 290–92; and Julianne Holt-Lunstad et al., "Loneliness and Social Isolation as Risk Factors for Mortality: A Meta-Analytic Review," *Perspectives on Psychological Science* 10, no. 2 (2015): 227.
- Gloria M.'s story was developed from a clinical encounter on January 15, 2008. Some of the story's details have been changed

to protect the identities of the parties involved.

• The Anchors Aweigh subsection was developed using material from David Schkade and Daniel Kahneman, "Does Living in California Make People Happy? A Focusing Illusion in Judgments of Life Satisfaction," *Psychological Science* 9, no. 5 (1998): 340–46; Zoltán Vass, *A Psychological Interpretation of Drawings and Paintings, The SSCA Method: A Systems Analysis Approach* (Budapest: Alexandra Publishing, 2011), 83; and Birte Englich and Kirsten Soder, "Moody Experts: How Mood and Expertise Influence Judgmental Anchoring," *Judgment and Decision Making* 4 (2009): 41–50.

• Material within the Powerless Communication subsection was adapted from Elliot Aronson et al., "The Effect of a Pratfall on Increasing Interpersonal Attractiveness," *Psychonomic Science* 4, no. 6 (1966): 227–28; Adam Grant, *Give and Take: A Revolutionary Approach to Success* (New York: Viking, 2013), 265; and Susan Cain, http://www.thepowerofintroverts. com/2013/07/04/7-ways-to-use-the-power-of-powerless-communication/ (accessed March 19, 2015).

CHAPTER THREE: *Humor*

• The Think Small story is adapted from: Andrea Hiott, *Thinking Small: The Long, Strange Trip of the Volkswagen Beetle* (New York: Ballantine, 2012), 1–16, 255–264, 338–345, 353–374; Dominik Imseng, *Think Small: The Story of the World's Greatest Ad* (Zurich, Switzerland: Full Stop Press, 2011), 60–74, 94–106; and Charles Gulas and Marc Weinberge, *Humor in Advertising: A Comprehensive Analysis* (Armonk, NY: M.E. Sharpe, 2006), 10.

• The Think Small number-one ad ranking came from a list at http://adage.com/article/special-report-the-advertising-century/ad-age-advertising-century-top-100-advertising-campaigns/140150/ (accessed January 1, 2015).

• E. B. White's quotation was found at http://en.wikiquote.org/ wiki/E._B._White (accessed May 12, 2015).

• Norman Cousins urged the scientific community to think about a connection between humor and health in his article "Anatomy of an Illness (as Perceived by the Patient)," *New England Journal of Medicine* 295 (1976): 1458–63.

- The material on humor's relationship to physical health was developed with the help of Rod A. Martin, *The Psychology of Humor: An Integrative Approach* (Waltham, MA: Academic Press, 2006), 309–33; and Sven Svebek, Solfrid Romundstad, and Jostein Holmen, "A 7-Year Prospective Study of Sense of Humor and Mortality in an Adult County Population: The Hunt-2 Study," *International Journal of Psychiatry in Medicine* 40 (2010): 125–46.

- Heart disease is the leading cause of death in the world, according to http://www.who.int/mediacentre/factsheets/fs310/en/ (accessed April 25, 2015).

- The Jewish joke about chicken soup was found at http://shortjewishgal.blogspot.com/2013/04/it-couldnt-hurt.html (accessed May 15, 2016).

- The Davies-Carr YouTube sensation story is adapted from: http://abcnews.go.com/Technology/charlie-bit-watched-youtube-clip-changed-familys-fortunes/story?id=16029675 (accessed April 29, 2015); http://www.nytimes.com/2012/02/10/world/europe/charlie-bit-my-finger-video-lifts-family-to-fame.html?_r=0 (accessed April 28, 2015); http://www.wsj.com/articles/SB100014240527 02303661904576454342874650316 (accessed April 28, 2015); and Jonah Berger and Katherine L. Milkman, "What Makes Online Content Viral?," *Journal of Marketing Research* 49 (2012): 192–05.

- Vivienne and Dan's story was developed through an interview on March 30, 2015 as well as several follow-up text messages, e-mails, and phone conversations.

- The material on laughter biology was derived from Robert Provine, *Laughter: A Scientific Investigation* (New York: Penguin, 2001), 36–53, 92–97; Pedro C. Marijuán and Jorge Navarro, "The Bonds of Laughter: A Multidisciplinary Inquiry into the Information Processes of Human Laughter," *BioInformation and Systems Biology Group Instituto Aragonés de Ciencias de la Salud 50009*

Zaragoza, Spain, http://arxiv.org/pdf/1010.5602.pdf (accessed
April 5, 2015); and Marshall Brain, "How Laughter Works,"
http://science.howstuffworks.com/life/inside-the-mind/emotions/
laughter.htm (accessed April 5, 2015).

• The notion of valuing humor in our romantic mates was studied by
Eric R. Bressler, Rod A. Martin, and Sigal Balshine, "Production
and Appreciation of Humor as Sexually Selected Qualities,"
Evolution and Human Behavior 27 (2006): 121–130.

• The value of humor in the workplace was adapted from
Jacquelyn Smith's *Forbes* article, http://www.forbes.
com/sites/jacquelynsmith/2013/05/03/10-reasons-why-
humor-is-a-key-to-success-at-work/ (accessed March 30,
2015), as well as surveys from CareerBuilder, http://www.
careerbuilder.com/share/aboutus/pressreleasesdetail.
aspx?sd=8%2F28%2F2013&id=pr778&ed=12%2F31%2F2013
(accessed March 30, 2015), and Accountemps, http://
accountemps.rhi.mediaroom.com/funny-business (accessed
March 30, 2015).

• The section on whether we truly value humor was developed
through http://www.bls.gov/tus/ (accessed May 25, 2015);
http://www.nielsen.com/us/en/insights/news/2011/10-years-
of-primetime-the-rise-of-reality-and-sports-programming.
html (accessed May 27, 2015); http://skift.com/2014/08/01/
comedy-is-the-most-popular-genre-in-the-in-flight-entertainment-
business/ (accessed May 28, 2015); http://www.boxofficemojo.
com/alltime/world/ (accessed May 28, 2015); http://www.
filmsite.org/bestpics2.html and http://oscar.go.com/blogs/oscar-
history (accessed May 28, 2015); http://www.theatlantic.com/
entertainment/archive/2012/01/why-do-the-oscars-hate-laugh-
out-loud-comedies/251985/#slide1 (accessed May 28, 2015);
and Sharon Lockyer and Lynn Myers, "It's About Expecting
the Unexpected: Live, Stand-Up Comedy from the Audience's
Perspective," *Journal of Audience and Reception Studies* 8
(2011): 172.

• The quotation from *Ferris Bueller's Day Off* was drawn from http://www.imdb.com/title/tt0091042/?ref_=ttqt_qt_tt (accessed April 10, 2015).

• Brenda Elsagher's story was adapted from her book *If the Battle Is Over, Why Am I Still in Uniform?* (Andover, MN: Expert Publishing, Inc., 2003) and through a telephone interview on December 14, 2015.

• The quotation from *Steel Magnolias* was drawn from http://www.imdb.com/title/tt0098384/quotes (accessed July 25, 2016).

• The material on humor's relationship to resiliency was developed from http://www.pbs.org/thisemotionallife/topic/humor/humor-and-resilience (accessed December 9, 2015); http://ejop.psychopen.eu/article/viewFile/464/354 (accessed December 9, 2015); and Rod A. Martin, *The Psychology of Humor: An Integrative Approach* (Waltham, MA: Academic Press, 2006), 269–307.

• Louie Anderson's quote about Wild Bill Bauer is found at http://www.twincities.com/ci_21436292/twin-cities-comic-wild-bill-bauer-dead-at (accessed December 20, 2015).

CHAPTER FOUR: *Spontaneity*

• The stories of Bob Sutherland, Cherry Republic, and the northern Michigan cherry crop devastation of 2012 were developed through an interview with Bob Sutherland on June 11, 2015 and an interview with Don Gregory on June 14, 2015. Additionally, several websites, accessed in late June 2015, provided useful details on adrenal cancer, the forces that drove the formation of the Great Lakes, stone fruit farming principles, and various contexts surrounding the cherry crop devastation: http://www.pbs.org/wgbh/nova/earth/cause-ice-age.html; http://www.glerl.noaa.gov/pr/ourlakes/background.html; http://www.great-lakes.net/teach/geog/lakeform/lf_1.html; http://cherryworks.net/about/history-of-cherries; http://rarediseases.info.nih.gov/gard/5751/adrenal-cancer/resources/1; http://www.pbs.org/newshour/updates/science-july-dec12-michigancherry_08-15; http://www.wzzm13.com/story/news/local/morning-features/2014/02/01/5120463/; http://www.wsj.com/articles/SB10001424052702304791709

4577420802349893464; and http://agilewriter.com/History/
CherryCapital.htm.

- The material on psychological flexibility is adapted from Todd
  B. Kashdan, "Psychological Flexibility as a Fundamental Aspect
  of Health," *Clinical Psychological Review* (November 1, 2010):
  865–78. Several experiments that were described in Kashdan's
  review, performed by outside parties, are also described in this
  chapter, namely, George A. Bonanno et al., "The Importance of
  Being Flexible: The Ability to Enhance and Suppress Emotional
  Expression Predicts Long-Term Adjustment," *Psychological
  Science* 157 (2004): 482–87; Sho Aoki et al., "Role of Striatal
  Cholinergic Interneurons in Set-Shifting in the Rat," *Journal
  of Neuroscience* (June 24, 2015): 9424–31; Robert Becklen
  and Daniel Cervone, "Selective Looking and the Noticing of
  Unexpected Events," *Memory & Cognition* 11 (1983): 601–08;
  Christopher Chabris and Daniel Simons, "Gorillas in Our
  Midst: Sustained Inattentional Blindness for Dynamic Events,"
  Perception 28 (1999): 1059–74; and Ulric Neisser, "The Control
  of Information Pickup in Selective Looking," in *Perception and
  Its Development: A Tribute to Eleanor J. Gibson*, ed. Anne D. Pick
  (Hillsdale, NJ: Lawrence Erlbaum Associates, 1979), 201–19.
- The stories of Lilian Bell and her Christmas Ship were developed
  through Lilian's personal account of the project that is presented
  in her book *The Story of the Christmas Ship* (Chicago: Rand
  McNally & Company, 1915); http://www.oldandsold.com/
  articles27n/women-authors-15.shtml (accessed September 2,
  2015); https://en.wikipedia.org/wiki/World_War_I (accessed
  September 10, 2015); and http://www.ibiblio.org/hyperwar/
  OnlineLibrary/photos/sh-usn/usnsh-j/ac12.htm (accessed
  September 12, 2015). Lilian's letter to the Children of America
  was edited for length, and fictitious names were added to the end
  of the letters from the children.
- Material on spontaneity associating with generosity as well as
  public-goods games was derived from the work of David Rand
  et al., "Spontaneous Giving and Calculated Greed," *Nature* 489

(September 20, 2012): 427–30.

- Samples translate into sales is detailed at http://www.theatlantic. com/business/archive/2014/10/the-psychology-behind-costcos-free-samples/380969/ (accessed August 4, 2016).
- The science of generosity was gathered from Christian Smith and Hilary Davidson, *The Paradox of Generosity: Giving We Receive, Grasping We Lose* (New York: Oxford, 2014), 44–45, 95, 99–113, 184.
- The origin of the phrase "Life is just a bowl of cherries" is described at https://en.wikipedia.org/wiki/Life_Is_Just_a_Bowl_of_Cherries (accessed September 20, 2015), and information on the revue *George White's Scandals* is described at https:// en.wikipedia.org/wiki/George_White%27s_Scandals (accessed September 20, 2015).

CHAPTER FIVE: *Wonder*

- Through a series of interviews in November and December 2015, Lisa and Brian Dover shared Ella's story with me. I am grateful for their openness and vulnerability during our conversations. I am also humbled by the trust they put in me to hold Ella's story sacred, while gently opening it for others to see and learn from. Ashley Jennings, Ella's nanny and angel-in-disguise, and Renee Shellhaas, MD, Ella's pediatric neurologist, provided valuable insights through e-mail and telephone correspondence in December 2015. In addition to Ashley and Dr. Shellhaas, many others have supported Lisa, Brian, and Ella through the years. They include, but are not limited to: Paula, Louis, Nancy, Tom, Kirsten, Jose, Sara, Anand, Brad, Sara-Marie, Kelly, Laurie, June, Lindsey, Mary, Denise, Kristine, Troy, Rachael, Jason, and Ellen. To all of you and many more, know that Lisa and Brian are grateful for your presence in their lives and consider each of you to be bright lights on the roads they have traveled . . . and the roads that are still to come.
- Information on subcortical band heterotopia was gathered from https://rarediseases.info.nih.gov/gard/1904/

subcortical-band-heterotopia/resources/1 (accessed November 17, 2015).

- The history of the ketogenic diet, including its rise, fall, and eventual rise again, is described in John M. Freeman et al., *The Ketogenic Diet: A Treatment for Children and Others with Epilepsy* (New York: Demos Medical Publishing, 2006), 19–36, and http://www.news-medical.net/health/History-of-the-Ketogenic-Diet.aspx (accessed November 15, 2015).

- Some of the medical information on cannabis oil is adapted from http://www.cnn.com/2013/08/07/health/charlotte-child-medical-marijuana/ (accessed November 22, 2015) and http://www.slate.com/articles/news_and_politics/altered_state/2014/02/how_dabbing_smoking_potent_hash_oil_could_blow_up_colorado_s_marijuana_legalization.html (accessed December 13, 2015).

- Material on the science of wonder, psychological concepts surrounding wonder, the benefits of wonder, John Muir, Walt Whitman, and Rachel Carson was adapted from Robert C. Fuller's inspiring book, *Wonder: From Emotion to Spirituality* (Chapel Hill, NC: University of North Carolina Press, 2006), 38–41, 44, 49, 102–109; http://www.ttbook.org/book/transcript/transcript-whats-wonder-jonathan-haidt (accessed November 10, 2015); http://www.huffingtonpost.com/jonathan-haidt/wonderful-versus-wonderfr_b_5022640.html (accessed November 10, 2015); http://www.slate.com/bigideas/why-do-we-feel-awe/essays-and-opinions/dacher-keltner-opinion (accessed November 10, 2015); http://www.huffingtonpost.com/2015/02/04/natural-anti-inflammatori_n_6613754.html (accessed November 10, 2015); http://www.rachelcarson.org (accessed November 11, 2015); and Rachel Carson's book *The Sense of Wonder* (New York: Harper & Row, 1956), 39, 42–43.

- Andrew Solomon's quote was taken from his stroke of genius *Far from the Tree: Parents, Children, and the Search for Identity* (New York: Scribner, 2013), 371.

- Glennon Doyle's piece about kairos time is from http://www.huffingtonpost.com/glennon-melton/dont-carpe-diem_b_1206346.

html (accessed December 4, 2015).

• Emily Perl Kingsley's background can be found at https://
en.wikipedia.org/wiki/Emily_Kingsley (accessed December 7,
2015). Her modern fable "Welcome to Holland" was first
published in Dear Abby's column "A Fable for Parents of a
Disabled Child," *Chicago Tribune*, November 5, 1989. Today, it
can be found on many different websites.

• Why we remember negative childhood experiences more than
positive ones is explained at http://www.nytimes.com/2012/03/24/
your-money/why-people-remember-negative-events-more-than-
positive-ones.html?_r=0 (accessed December 10, 2015).

CONCLUSION: *The Rainbow Hallway*

• Some minor details of Eleanor Schaeffer's anecdote have been
changed to protect the identities of the parties involved.

• David Brooks's thoughts on virtues can be found at http://www.
nytimes.com/2015/04/12/opinion/sunday/david-brooks-the-moral-
bucket-list.html?_r=0 (accessed December 29, 2015) and https://
www.ted.com/talks/david_brooks_should_you_live_for_your_
resume_or_your_eulogy?language=en (accessed December 29,
2015).

• Information on mirror neurons can be found at http://www.apa.org/
monitor/oct05/mirror.aspx (accessed December 30, 2015).

About the Author

Anthony T. DeBenedet, M.D. is a practicing physician and behavioral-science enthusiast. His interviews and writings have run in various media outlets, including the *New York Times*, the *Today* show, the *Washington Post*, and *TIME Ideas*. He also co-authored *The Art of Rough-housing: Good Old-Fashioned Horseplay and Why Every Kid Needs It* (Quirk Books, 2011), a parenting book about the importance of parent–child physical play.

DeBenedet has a Bachelor of Science Degree in Biomedical Engineering from the Duke University Pratt School of Engineering, a Master of Science Degree in Health and Healthcare Research from the University of Michigan Rackham Graduate School, and a Doctor of Medicine Degree from the University of Virginia School of Medicine. He completed his internal medicine residency and gastroenterology fellowship at the University of Michigan Health System.

DeBenedet lives in Ann Arbor, Michigan, where he enjoys spending time with his family, connecting with friends, and playing a little basketball.